Dedication

To Robbin Bedard, a terrific friend.

Acknowledgments

I would like to thank acquisitions editor
Julie Stephani, editor Maria Turner, and
page designer Donna Mummery at
Krause Publications for helping me
make this book a reality.
I am also grateful to photographer Kevin Dilley
for the stunning photographs and to
illustrator Cherie Hanson for the excellent
diagrams and illustrations.
Finally, thank you to Ann Gladwell for use of her
beautiful home as a backdrop for my projects.

Table of Contents

Introduction

Over the years, I have discovered and rediscovered many art supplies and crafting techniques. I dabble in some, like batik, and become totally engrossed in others, like silk screening, strip piecing, weaving, and jewelry making to name a few.

Anyway, my best friend lives halfway across the country, so we do most of our communicating by phone. Every few months, I will announce something like, "Tile glazing is my favorite thing!" That is her cue to say, "I thought paper crafting was your favorite thing." Then I have to qualify my statement: "OK then, it's my *new* favorite thing."

I am happy to say that for the past year, felt has been my new favorite old thing—or my new old favorite thing. Felt is the best stuff ever.

When I began making projects for this book, I intended to make several penny rugs. I love the graphic nature of penny rugs. They become miniature color studies—a version of early American pop art. Although these rugs were originally made from boiled wool, they can also be made from felt. Felt won't fray, it is easy to layer and to stitch around, and it comes in a wide variety of colors.

I love penny rugs, but I never got around to making any because I was too busy shaping and manipulating felt in ways that I hadn't tried before. There were many experiments that didn't work, such as "aging" ivory felt by crinkling it up and dipping it in watered-down brown paint. This turned out dingy and depressing, and felt doesn't really crinkle. Another failed experiment involved weaving fine strips of felt on a mini-loom; the strips fell apart.

But there were many techniques that worked and the results are terrific! Of course, you can stitch, glue, and stuff felt—but did you know that you can stamp, fuse, smock, stencil, coil, sculpt, and make yo-yos with it? You can even use decorator chalk used for scrapbooking to color felt.

Felt is a humble, inexpensive fiber that can be dressed-up and transformed into sophisticated and stylized home accents. After trying some of these techniques, it will become your new old favorite, too.

Most projects are easy enough for those of beginning to intermediate skill levels. The most difficult project to execute is the Spiral and Leaf Coiled Frame, page 74. It takes a few minutes of practice to roll and shape the felt strips, but once you master the technique, you will want to make more.

Since the focus of the book is on home decorating items, there are many throw pillows. All of the techniques, used to make the pillows can be adapted for other home dec items or can even be incorporated into clothing.

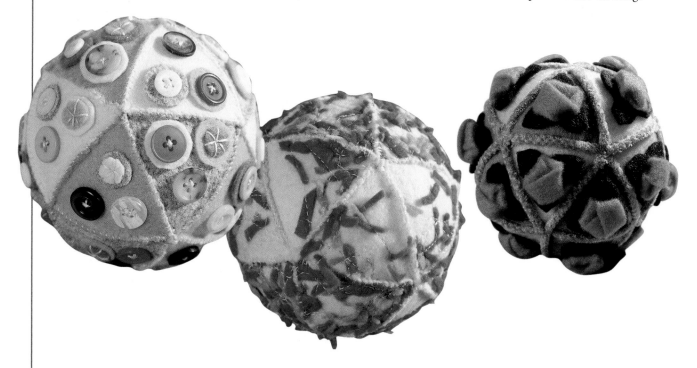

chapter one

General Instructions

About Felt

Felt is a non-woven textile made of fibers that are matted together. Since the fibers are small and entwine in all directions, it has a flat matte finish that absorbs light and has no grain. It has been made for thousands of years. Before spinning and weaving, there was felt-making. The ancients used wool fibers to make felt, which resulted in a material that was warm enough for coats and sturdy enough for tent walls. Joseph's coat of many colors may have been made from wool felt that was dyed with intense vegetable and metallic dyes.

Most felt available in craft and fabric stores is 100% acrylic. It is offered in 9" x 12" pre-cut rectangles, 36" packaged squares, or rolled on a bolt. Felt is also available in blends of 20% to 30% wool and rayon. The projects made from wool blend felt include: the Mission Pillows, pages 46 through 50; the Four-Window Pillow, page 14; and the Crazy Quilt Wall Hanging/Throw, page 124. Wool blend felt can be washed to achieve a bumpy or dimpled surface. After washing, it becomes very soft to the touch, and it is lightweight enough to use in clothing.

When comparing different styles and brands of felt, you will notice that it varies in weight and hand. It can be flat and stiff, or full and soft. Felt of average density works best for the projects contained within this book. For instance, felt that is too flat doesn't coil well, and felt that is too full, doesn't stamp well. After working with various weights, you will find which ones work best for your favorite techniques.

Whipstitching

Whipstitching is simply joining two or more layers together with a simple wrapping stitch.

When whipstitching the front and back together of a shape that will be stuffed, it is necessary to have stitches tightly spaced, as shown below.

When tacking two layers of fabric together, or attaching a three-dimensional surface decoration to fabric, the stitches can be more widely spaced, as shown below.

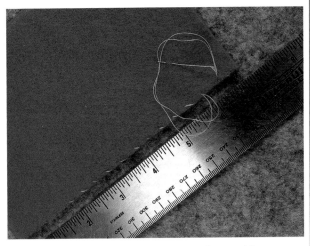

Embroidery Stitches

Several embroidery stitches are used in various projects throughout this book. Here, I have detailed simple steps for completing each, as well as helpful diagrams so you can see how each stitch is accomplished. If you are unfamiliar with any of the stitches, it is probably best to practice each on scrap felt or material before trying them on the actual projects.

Backstitch

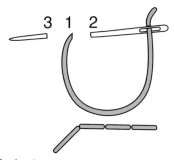

The backstitch is used for line work or outlining.

Begin by bringing the needle up at 1 as shown in the diagram, down at 2, and up again at 3. Return to 1 and continue.

Wrapped Backstitch

After backstitching, working left to right, insert needle through first stitch, wrap and insert needle through second stitch. Continue in same manner.

Chain Stitch

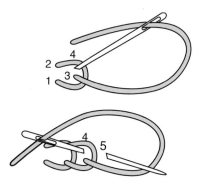

After bringing the needle up at 1 in the diagram, form a small loop of thread and hold in place with left thumb. (Use right thumb if you are stitching with your left hand.)

Insert needle at 2.

Bring needle up at 3 inside first loop to form second loop. Hold with thumb and insert needle at 4.

Repeat to form a chain.

Secure the end with a small stitch over last loop.

French Knot

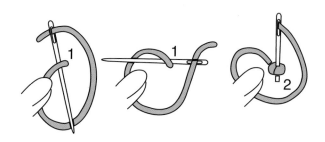

Bring needle up and wrap floss once around it. (For a fuller knot, wrap floss around needle twice.)

Insert the needle in fabric nest to where it was brought up initially and pull taught.

Long Stitch

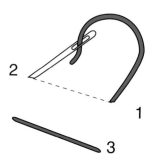

This stitch is used on the Button Ball and Cross-Hatched Hearts projects, pages 84 and 115.

While referring to the diagram, come up; at 1 and down at 2. Continue this parallel stitch by coming up through 3 and so on. The length of stitch will vary depending on design.

Couched Long Stitch

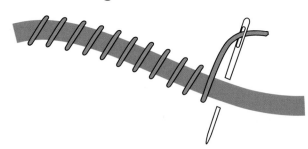

Use a series of even short stitches to secure trim or ribbon in place.

Running Stitch

Working right to left (if right-handed), simply stitch up and down, generally in a straight line. Be sure to stitch through all layers.

Satin Stitch

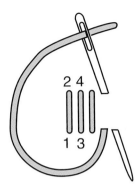

The satin stitch is used to fill in a shape with a solid ground of floss.

Begin by coming up at 1, as shown in the diagram, and continue down at 2. Repeat with parallel stitches. Make sure tension is even for each stitch to create flat or "satin" surface.

Star Stitch

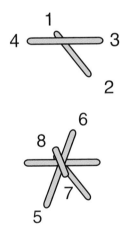

This stitch is used in the centers of circles on the Floral Appliqued Frame, page 66.

While referring to the diagram, begin by bringing the needle up at 1, down at 2, up at 3, and down at 4. Continue with the needle coming up again at 5, down at 6, up at 7, and down at 8.

Stem Stitch

This stitch is used for line work or outlining.

While referring to the diagram, come up at 1, down at 2, up at 3, and down at 4. Continue in the same manner.

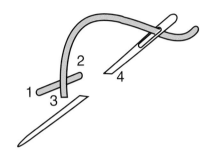

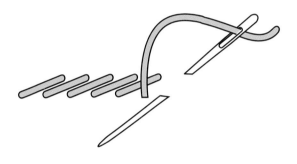

Mitered Corners

A mitered corner has a 45-degree seam where borders meet. This diagonal seam provides a visually satisfying frame around a center design.

1. At the corner, machine stitch each border strip to within ¼" of the edge of center square.

2. Right sides together, fold fabric at a 45-degree angle.

3. With ruler, mark line that continues from edge to corners of borders, and pin.

4. Machine stitch on marked line, meeting at stopping point of border seams.

5. Trim and press.

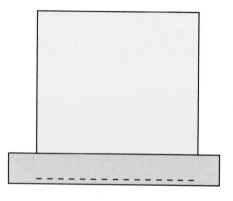

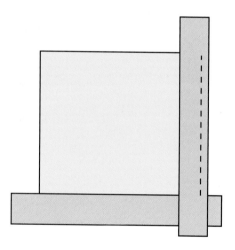

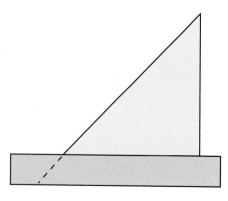

Trimming Corners

To reduce bulk at corners, trim diagonally through both layers.

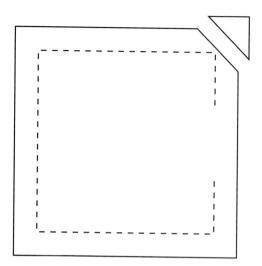

Trimming and Pressing Checkerboard Piecing

Piecing with felt adds bulk. To make pieced sections lay flatter, trim at intersections and press felt sections toward cotton squares.

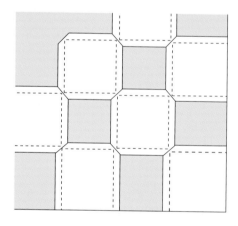

Hand Appliqué

1. Pin or baste shape to background fabric.

2. Hand stitch shape to background fabric using tiny evenly spaced stitches.

3. To make stitches less visible, insert the needle through both layers, then down through felt, very close to where you last came up.

4. "Carry" thread on the wrong side and make next stitch.

5. Knot at back.

Stenciling

Felt has a slight "tooth" that allows it to receive paint well. Since it is non-woven and is thicker than paper or cotton fabric, it can absorb more paint. However, use only enough paint to create the image, as too much will make the fabric stiff and the overall design less attractive.

The materials lists for the stencil projects call for Mylar. This is lightweight plastic that can be cut with a craft knife. Stencil blanks, uncut sheets of plastic used to make commercial stencils, are available at craft stores. They work well but are more opaque than clear sheets of Mylar. I often cut up lightweight plastic folders, binders, and even page protectors. They are transparent and the perfect size for most projects.

Make a separate stencil for each color.

1. Trace design on white paper.

2. With permanent marker, trace design on Mylar, as shown below.

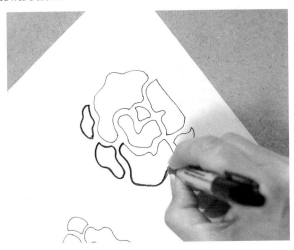

3. Place on cutting surface and with craft knife, cut out each marked section, as shown.

4. Position stencil on felt. Apply small amount of paint to stencil brush. On scrap paper, remove excess paint with a circular motion, as shown.

5. Holding brush perpendicular to felt surface and lightly touching felt with brush, apply paint in a pouncing motion, as shown below.

Be sure to hold stencil firmly in place while applying paint, as shown, to ensure a crisp edge.

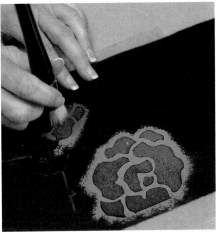

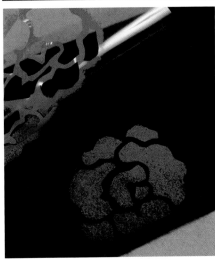

chapter two

Head For the Pillows

Without a doubt, a throw pillow is the definitive decorating accessory. Several years ago, I worked as an interior designer, and I quickly learned how important these ubiquitous accents are to a room. A few knockout throw pillows tossed on a sofa or bed can give any interior space a quick face-lift. Pillows can also dress up small niches such as bookshelves or windowsills. This chapter offers a variety of felt pillows with interesting hues and textures. Make them to dress up your own home, or wrap them up as exceptional gifts for exceptional friends.

❖ ½-yard purple wool felt
  (20% wool/80% rayon)
❖ 9" x 12" cut blue/gray felt
❖ 9" x 12" cut lavender felt
❖ 9" x 12" cut dark purple felt
❖ ⅛-yard green print cotton fabric
❖ Blue/gray thread
❖ Dark purple thread
❖ Lavender thread
❖ Fiberfill
❖ Sewing machine
❖ Iron

All seam allowances are ¼".

Four-Window Pillow

The design for this pillow was adapted from a traditional quilt pattern called the Cathedral Window. It appears complex, but it is actually much easier to execute in felt, than in traditional cotton fabric. Since felt doesn't fray, as does cotton, it is not necessary to turn the raw edges under, or to hide them in a seam. The curved windows are layered on top of a simple checkerboard design, for an easy way to achieve a striking effect. Start with the Four-Window Pillow, then make the companion Sixteen-Window Pillow. Finally, impress your friends and acquaintances by graduating to the Twenty-Five-Window Pillow.

1. Cut 3½" squares as follows:
   ❖ Five from blue/gray felt.
   ❖ Four from green print fabric.

2. Right sides together and with blue/gray thread, machine stitch squares together, starting and stopping ¼" from ends of squares, as shown in Diagram A. Form checkerboard with

felt corners and press. (See General Instructions for Trimming and Pressing Checkerboards, page 10.)

3. From lavender felt, cut four Pattern A shapes.

4. From dark purple felt, cut four Pattern B shapes.

Diagram A

5. Matching dots to seams, place A-shapes on checkerboard, as shown in Diagram B.

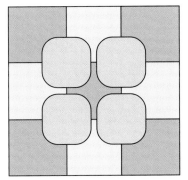

Diagram B

6. Matching points to dots, place B-shapes on A-shapes, as shown in Diagram C.

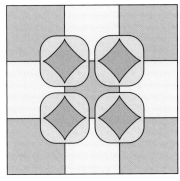

Diagram C

7. Pin or baste through all layers and with dark purple thread, machine stitch along stitching lines, as shown in Diagram D. Remove basting stitches if necessary.

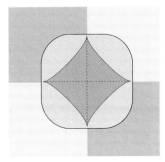

Diagram D

8. Fold curves of A-shapes toward center and pin in place. With lavender thread, whipstitch curves in place. See photo below for guidance.

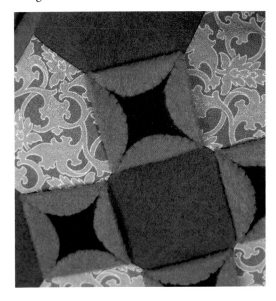

9. From purple wool felt, cut four 2" x 13" strips.

10. Right sides together, center strips to sides of checkerboard. With purple thread, machine stitch strips to checkerboard, starting and stopping seams ¼" from ends. Miter corners. (Refer to General Instructions for Mitered Corners, page 10.) Press.

11. From purple wool felt, cut one 13" square for pillow back.

12. Wrong sides together with purple thread, machine stitch pillow top to pillow back ¾" in from cut edge, leaving opening to insert fiberfill.

13. Lightly stuff pillow with fiberfill.

14. Pin and machine stitch seam to complete. Trim through both layers ½" from seam.

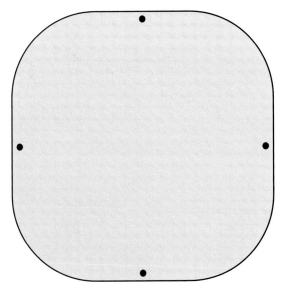

Pattern A

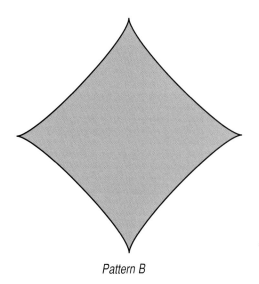

Pattern B

❖ ½-yard olive green felt
❖ 2 cuts dark purple felt
   (each 9" x 12")
❖ ⅛-yard dark blue print
   cotton fabric
❖ ⅛-yard burgundy print
   cotton fabric
❖ Dark blue thread
❖ Dark purple thread
❖ 14" pillow form
❖ Sewing machine
❖ Iron

All seam allowances are ¼".

Sixteen-Window Pillow

A companion to the Four-Window Pillow, the windows on this pillow extend from edge to edge.

1. Cut 3½" squares as follows:
   ❖ 13 from green felt.
   ❖ 12 from blue print fabric.

2. Right sides together and with dark blue thread, machine stitch squares together, starting and stopping ¼" from ends of squares, as shown in Diagram A. Form checkerboard with felt squares in corners and press. (See General Instructions for Trimming and Pressing Checkerboards, page 10.)

Diagram A

3. From dark purple felt, cut 16 Pattern A shapes.

4. From burgundy fabric, cut 16 Pattern B shapes.

5. Matching dots to seams, place A-shapes on checkerboard, as shown in Diagram B.

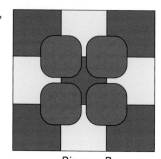

Diagram B

6. Matching points to dots, place B shapes on A-shapes, as shown in Diagram C.

7. Pin or baste through all layers and with dark purple thread, machine stitch along stitching lines, as shown in Diagram D. Remove basting stitches if necessary.

8. Fold curves of A-shapes toward center and pin in place. With dark purple thread, whipstitch curves in place, as shown in step 8 of the Four-Window Pillow project, page 15.

9. From green felt, cut one 15½" square for pillow back.

10. Right sides together with blue thread, machine stitch front to back leaving opening to insert pillow form. Trim excess fabric from corners. (Refer to General Instructions for Trimming Corners, page 10.)

11. Turn right-side out and insert pillow form.

12. With blue thread, whipstitch opening closed.

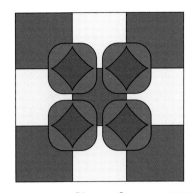

Diagram C

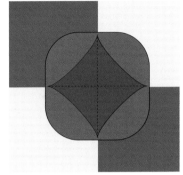

Diagram D

Note: Since pillow forms do not come in 15" sizes, the finished size of the pre-stuffed pillow, the materials list calls for a 14" form. Fiberfill may be added if desired for a plumper pillow.

Pattern A

Pattern B

* ½-yard butterscotch felt
* ¼-yard dusty pink felt
* 9" x 12" cut ivory felt
* ⅛-yard gold moiré fabric
* Ivory thread
* Dusty pink thread
* 14" pillow form
* Sewing machine

All seam allowances are ¼".

Twenty-five-Window Pillow

Once the first layer of 16 windows is in place, the remaining nine windows fit logically in between. Look closely at centers to notice subtle changes in color and texture. This window-covered pillow will definitely light up a room.

1. From butterscotch felt, cut two 14½" squares for pillow top and back.

2. From pink felt, cut 25 Pattern A shapes.

3. From gold moiré fabric, cut 16 Pattern B shapes.

4. Center and pin 16 Pattern A shapes to pillow top. Arrange in four rows of four with ¼" between each shape.

5. According to Diagram A, match points to dots and place gold moiré B-shapes on top of A-shapes.

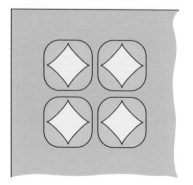

Diagram A

6. Pin or baste through all layers and with ivory thread, machine stitch from top to bottom and from side to side of each B-shape, as shown in the photo at right. Remove basting stitches, if necessary.

7. Fold curves of A-shapes toward center, pin in place, and with pink thread, whipstitch curves in place.

8. From ivory felt, cut nine Pattern B shapes.

9. According to Diagram B, center remaining nine pink A-shapes between stitched diamonds and pin in place on pillow top.

Diagram B

10. According to Diagram C, match points to dots and place ivory felt B-shapes on A-shapes.

11. Pin or baste through all layers and with ivory thread, machine stitch from top to bottom and from side to side of each B-shape, as in step 6. Remove basting stitches, if necessary.

Diagram C

12. Fold curves of A-shapes toward center, pin in place, and with pink thread, whipstitch curves in place.

13. Right sides together, machine stitch pillow front to pillow back, leaving opening to insert pillow form. Trim excess fabric from corners. (Refer to General Instructions for Trimming Corners, page 10.)

14. Turn right-side out, insert pillow form, and whipstitch opening closed.

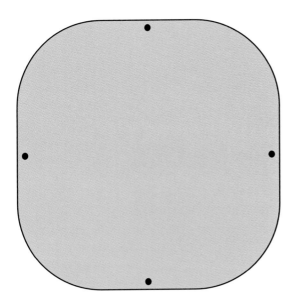

Pattern A

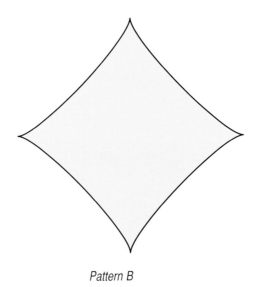

Pattern B

- ⅓-yard cream felt
- ⅓-yard textured cotton fabric
- ½-yard cream cotton fabric for back
- 1¾ yards covered cording
- 12" pillow form
- Cream thread
- Red thread
- Leaf rubber stamp
- Brown waterproof ink dye pad
- Green waterproof ink dye pad
- ⅓-yard water-soluble stabilizer (such as Solvy)
- Water-soluble marking pen
- Sewing machine
- Iron

All seam allowances are ¼".

Embroidered Bird Pillow

In the mid-1800s, Turkish rug makers cooked up a remarkable red dye. Cotton rug fibers were dyed a vibrant crimson that wouldn't fade after washing or exposure to the sun. Soon this red cotton thread traveled across Europe from Turkey to Germany, where German women used it for embroidery work. "Redwork," as it came to be known, was characterized by simple linear designs worked in red thread with running or stem stitches. This form of stitchery was introduced in America by immigrating Germans and was popular until around 1920, when a rainbow of colorfast dyes were developed.

This pillow combines the contemporary art of stamping with an updated version of redwork. This redwork is created in no time as it is machine stitched. Felt serves as the perfect "canvas" for both techniques, since it is porous enough to absorb stamping ink and sturdy enough for machine satin stitching.

1. From cream felt, cut one 9½" square.

2. With stamp and brown ink, stamp design onto cream felt square in random pattern and let dry. Repeat with green ink. Let dry.

3. With marker and using the template on page 24, transfer bird design to stabilizer.

4. Pin or baste stabilizer to stamped felt.

5. Adjust sewing machine to ³⁄₃₂"-wide satin stitch and with red thread, machine satin stitch over marked pattern. Trim threads.

6. Carefully tear or trim away large areas of stabilizer. To remove remaining stabilizer, follow manufacturer's directions and submerge in water. Let dry. Remove basting stitches if necessary.

7. From textured fabric, cut four 2½" x 13½" strips for border.

8. Right sides together, center and pin strips to sides of felt.

9. With cream thread, machine stitch strips to felt, starting and stopping seams ¼" from ends. Miter corners. (Refer to General Instructions for Mitered Corners, page 10.) Press.

10. From cream cotton fabric, cut one 13½" square for pillow back.

11. Matching raw edges, use cream thread to machine stitch covered cording to pillow front, ¼" in from edge. Overlap ends, as shown in Diagram A.

12. Right sides together and using cream thread, machine stitch pillow front to pillow back, leaving opening to insert pillow form. Trim excess fabric from corners. (Refer to General Instructions for Trimming Corners, page 10.)

13. Turn right-side out, insert pillow form, and whipstitch opening closed with cream thread.

Diagram A

materials needed

- ⅓-yard cream felt
- ⅓-yard textured cotton fabric
- ½-yard cream cotton fabric for back
- 1¾ yards covered cording
- 12" pillow form
- Cream thread
- Red thread
- Leaf rubber stamp
- Brown waterproof ink dye pad
- Green waterproof ink dye pad
- ⅓-yard water-soluble stabilizer (such as Solvy)
- Water-soluble marking pen
- Sewing machine

All seam allowances are ¼".

Embroidered Floral Pillow

This pillow is a companion to the Embroidered Bird Pillow. Make one or both variations to sit at the head of your bed or to pad your antique settee.

1. From cream felt, cut one 9½" square.

2. With stamp and brown ink, stamp design onto cream felt square in random pattern and let dry. Repeat with green ink. Let dry.

3. With marker and using the template on page 25, transfer floral design to stabilizer.

4. Pin or baste stabilizer to stamped felt.

5. Adjust sewing machine to ³⁄₃₂"-wide satin stitch and with red thread, machine satin stitch over marked pattern. Trim threads.

6. Carefully tear or trim away large areas of stabilizer. To remove remaining stabilizer, follow manufacturer's directions and submerge in water. Let dry. Remove basting stitches if necessary.

7. From textured fabric, cut four 2½" x 13½" strips for border.

8. Right sides together, center and pin strips to sides of felt.

9. With cream thread, machine stitch strips to felt, starting and stopping seams ¼" from ends. Miter corners. (Refer to General Instructions for Mitered Corners, page 10.) Press.

10. From cream cotton fabric, cut one 13½" square for pillow back.

11. Matching raw edges, use cream thread to machine stitch covered cording to pillow front, ¼" in from edge. Overlap ends, as shown in Diagram A.

12. Right sides together and using cream thread, machine stitch pillow front to pillow back, leaving opening to insert pillow form. Trim excess fabric from corners. (Refer to General Instructions for Trimming Corners, page 10.)

13. Turn right-side out, insert pillow form, and whipstitch opening closed with cream thread.

Diagram A

Embroidered Bird Pillow
Bird Design Template

Embroidered Floral Pillow
Floral Design Template

- ⅓-yard purple felt
- 9" x 12" sage green felt cut
- 1¾ yards gold velvet ribbon (⅞" wide)
- 9 buttons (¹¹⁄₁₆" size)
- Gold thread
- Purple thread
- Sage green thread
- 1½ yards cotton fringe
- Fiberfill
- Sewing machine

All seam allowances are ¼".

Ribbon Pillow

After an afternoon of folding colored paper strips for collages, I decided to try the same folding techniques with felt. Bold strips cut from felt and wrapped with folded ribbon, combine to make this upscale pillow. The antique black buttons and the thick cotton fringe provide the perfect finishing touches.

1. From purple felt, cut two 11½" x 14½" rectangles for pillow front and back.

2. From green felt, cut three Pattern A shapes using the template on the facing page.

3. Pin or baste shapes to one rectangle, as shown in Diagram A.

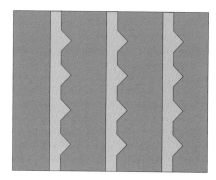

Diagram A

4. With green thread, whipstitch the three A-shape pieces of felt to pillow top, only on both sides of "points."

5. From ribbon, cut three 21" lengths.

6. Working right to left with one length of ribbon, thread diagonally under one felt shape from the bottom up. Pin in place, fold ribbon, and again thread under felt shape. Complete threading, folding, and pinning along entire length of felt shape.

7. With gold thread, whipstitch ribbon to pillow top, as shown.

8. Repeat the ribbon-threading process described above on the other two felt shapes.

9. With gold thread, hand stitch buttons to pillow top, as shown.

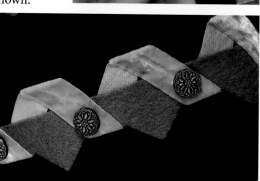

10. Turn fringe to inside of pillow top and matching bound edge of fringe to raw edge of pillow top, pin or baste in place.

11. Right sides together and with purple thread, machine stitch front to back leaving opening to insert fiberfill. Trim excess fabric from corners. (Refer General Instructions for Trimming Corners, page 10.)

12. Turn right-side out, insert fiberfill, and whipstitch opening closed with purple thread.

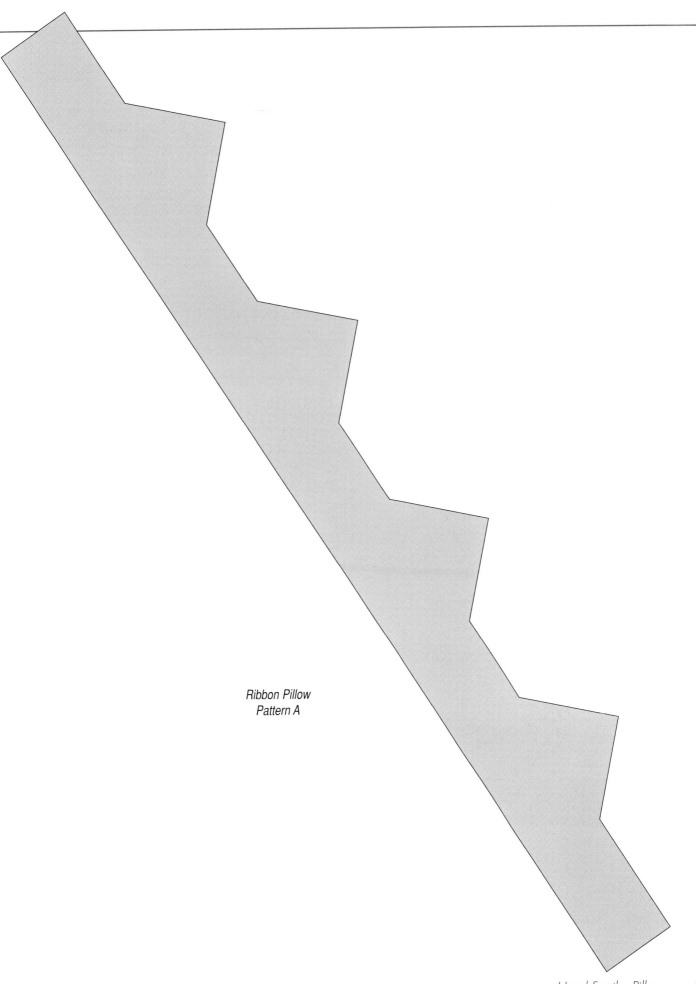

Ribbon Pillow
Pattern A

❖ ½-yard butterscotch felt
❖ ⅓-yard tan felt
❖ ⅓-yard cotton fabric for lining
❖ Butterscotch thread
❖ 13 yellow wooden beads
❖ 3 blue wooden beads
❖ 3 skeins embroidery floss
   in colors to coordinate with
   bead colors
❖ Ruler
❖ Air-soluble marking pen
❖ 10" pillow form
❖ Sewing machine

All seam allowances are ¼".

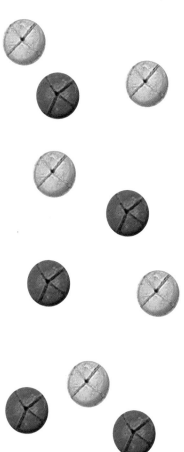

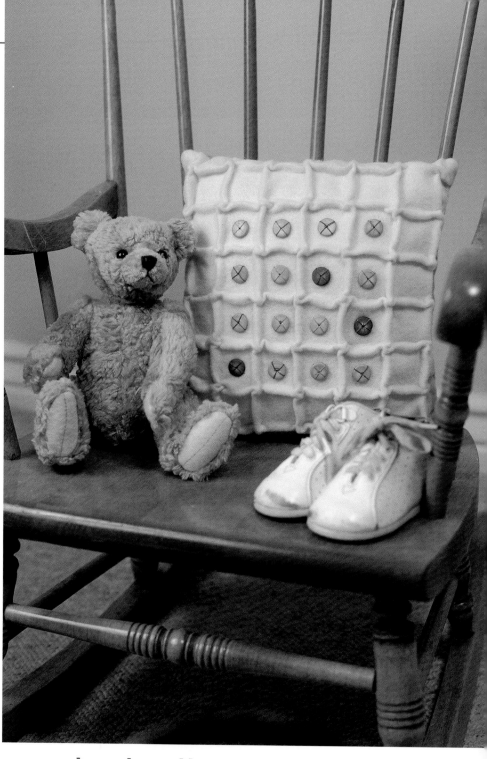

Smocked Pillow

Smocking is a fabric manipulation process that is worked in small, measured pleats or puckers. It was traditionally used on yokes and sleeves of linen clothing to add decoration or volume. An ancient craft, it can be seen on the garments worn by people portrayed in Medieval and Renaissance paintings.

Since felt is bulkier than fine linen, this version is done on a large scale and made into a simple square pillow. Working on the wrong side of the fabric, use large stitches to quickly transform a flat piece of soft felt into a three-dimensional windowpane design.

1. From butterscotch felt, cut one 15" square.

2. With marking pen, mark for smocking, as shown in Diagram A. Repeat dots A through D seven times down and seven times across.

3. To smock, start at A, go to B, then C, then D, and back to A, as illustrated in Diagram B. Pull thread tightly, and knot to secure. Repeat to finish entire area of pillow top.

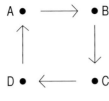

Diagram B

4. Trim smocked felt to 10½".

5. Cut lining fabric to 10½".

6. With wrong sides together, machine stitch lining fabric to smocked felt ¼" from raw edge.

7. With two strands of floss, hand stitch beads to centers of recessed squares.

8. From tan felt, cut one 10½" square for pillow back.

9. Right sides together, machine stitch pillow front to pillow back, leaving opening to insert pillow form. Trim excess fabric from corners. (Refer to General Instructions for Trimming Corners, page 10.)

10. Turn right-side out, insert pillow form, and whipstitch opening closed.

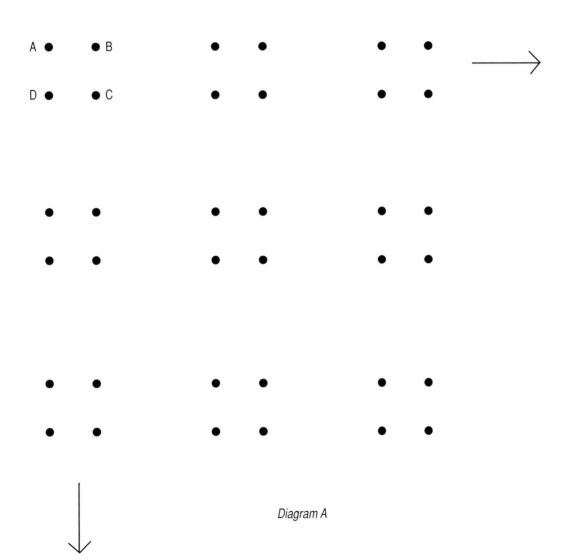

Diagram A

Leaf It to Felt

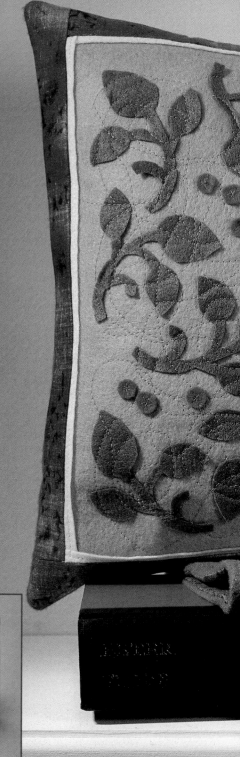

The common theme of this eclectic offering of projects is felt foliage. Bring the outside in and pay homage to Mother Nature with felt flora that won't fade or wilt.

❖ ½-yard tan felt
❖ ⅓-yard sage green felt
❖ 9" x 12" cut ivory felt
❖ 9" x 12" cut lavender felt
❖ ⅓-yard water-soluble stabilizer
❖ ¼-yard purple print cotton fabric
❖ ½-yard gray felt
❖ Tan thread
❖ Purple thread
❖ Ivory thread
❖ 14" pillow form
❖ Sewing machine
❖ Iron

All seam allowances are ¼".

Leaf Puzzle Pillow

One of the most intriguing and satisfying methods of machine appliqué is done with one continuous stitched seam that winds back and forth to create a serpentine network of thread. This delicate network secures the leaves and berries beneath it. (Felt is the fabric of choice for these shapes because there are no raw edges to finish.) The labyrinth of machine stitching creates a very subtle design within a design.

Try other simple silhouette shapes for the surface design, such as fish or clouds.

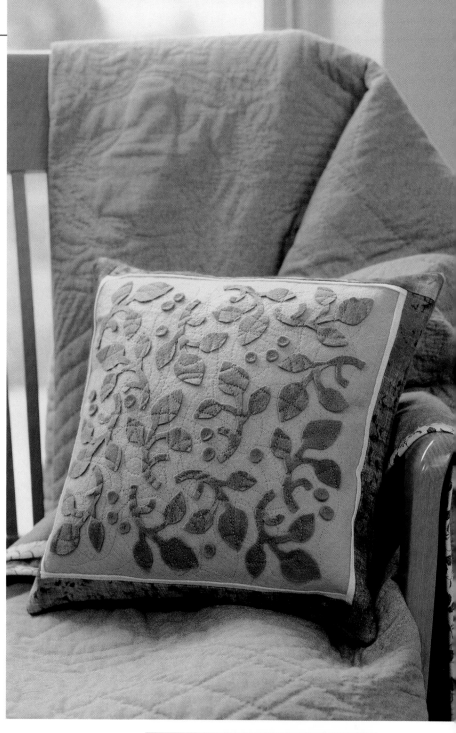

1. From tan felt, cut one 13" square for pillow top.

2. From green felt, cut 14 leaf sprigs with Pattern A.

3. Place sprigs on felt square, as shown in Diagram A.

4. From stabilizer, cut one 12" square.

5. Place stabilizer over arranged sprigs and carefully baste through all layers.

Diagram A

6. With tan thread and one continuous seam, machine stitch in random curve pattern, as shown below. Make enough passes back and forth on the square to secure all leaves and stems.

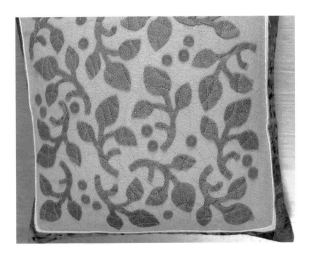

7. Following manufacturer's directions, remove stabilizer by submerging square in water. Let dry.

8. Trim square to 12".

9. From lavender felt, cut 18 ½" circles using Pattern B.

10. Referring to Diagram A as a guide, pin the 18 circles to tan felt square and with one strand of lavender embroidery floss, hand stitch lavender circles to square, as shown in Diagram B.

Diagram B

11. From ivory felt, cut four ¾" x 12" strips.

12. Matching raw edges, and overlapping at corners, pin or baste strips to outside edge of square, as shown in Diagram C.

13. With tan thread, machine stitch strips to border. Remove basting stitches if necessary.

14. From purple print fabric, cut four 1¾" x 13¼" strips for border.

15. Right sides together and using purple thread, machine stitch first strip to center square, stopping seam ¼" from edge of square, as shown in Diagram D. Press. Continue with remaining strips.

16. Tuck short end of last strip, under first strip. Complete seam from first strip, as shown in Diagram E. Press.

17. From gray felt, cut one 14½" square for pillow back.

18. Right sides together and with purple thread, machine stitch front to back leaving opening to insert pillow form. Trim excess fabric from corners. (See General Instructions for Trimming Corners, page 10.)

19. Turn right-side out, insert pillow form, and whipstitch opening closed with purple thread.

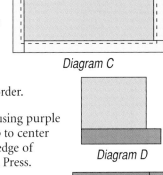

Diagram C

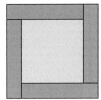

Diagram D

Diagram E

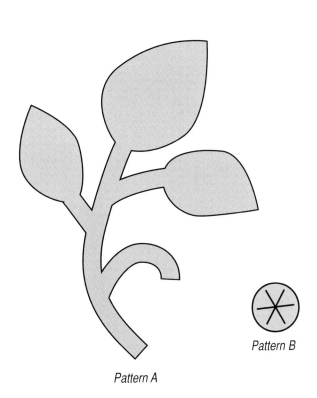

Pattern A

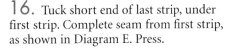

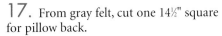

Pattern B

❖ ½-yard butterscotch felt
❖ ⅓-yard sage green felt
❖ 9" x 12" cut lavender felt
❖ ⅓-yard water-soluble stabilizer
❖ ½-yard gray felt
❖ ¾-yard gray print cotton fabric
❖ Yellow thread
❖ Lavender thread
❖ Gray thread
❖ ¾-yard rayon fringe
❖ Sewing machine
❖ Iron
❖ Masking tape (optional)

All seam allowances are ¼".

Leaf Puzzle Table Runner

A companion piece for the Leaf Puzzle Pillow, this runner is designed to show off the all-over leaf design on any table size or shape. This runner can also grace a dresser or a mantle.

1. From butterscotch felt, cut one 13" square for one runner end.

2. Using Pattern A on facing page, cut 14 leaf sprigs from green felt.

3. Referring to Diagram A from Leaf Puzzle Pillow, place sprigs on felt square.

4. From stabilizer, cut one 12" square.

5. Place stabilizer over arranged sprigs and carefully baste through all layers.

Diagram A

6. With tan thread and one continuous seam, machine stitch in random curve pattern, as shown below. Make enough passes back and forth on the square to secure all leaves and stems.

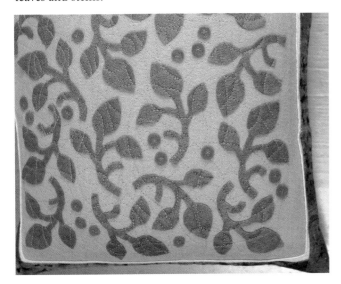

7. Following manufacturer's directions, remove stabilizer by submerging square in water. Let dry.

8. Trim square to 12".

9. From lavender felt, cut 18 ½" circles using Pattern B.

10. Referring to Diagram A as a guide, pin the 18 circles to butterscotch felt square and with one strand of lavender embroidery floss, hand stitch lavender circles to square, as shown in Diagram B.

Diagram B

11. Repeat steps 1 through 10 for other runner end.

12. From gray felt, cut one 11½" x 35" rectangle.

13. Right sides together and with gray thread, machine stitch appliquéd butterscotch ends to short sides of gray rectangle.

14. From rayon fringe, cut two 11½" lengths.

15. Turn fringe to inside of table runner and matching bound edge of fringe to end of table runner, pin or baste in place. To secure fringe while machine stitching, tape or baste to appliquéd ends.

16. From gray print fabric, cut one 11½" x 58" rectangle for runner back.

17. Right sides together and with gray thread, machine stitch runner top to runner back, leaving 6" opening to turn. Trim excess fabric from corners. (Refer to General Instructions for Trimming Corners, page 10.)

18. Turn right-side out, remove tape or basting stitches, and whipstitch opening closed with gray thread. Press.

Pattern B

Pattern A

- ❖ 3 cuts bright pink felt (9" x 12")
- ❖ ⅛-yard green print fabric
- ❖ ⅛-yard fusible web
- ❖ Bright pink thread
- ❖ Green thread
- ❖ 9 feet 32-gauge green wire
- ❖ 8" Styrofoam wreath
- ❖ 1 package dried green moss
- ❖ Hot glue gun and glue sticks
- ❖ ⅔-yard twine
- ❖ Iron

Rose Wreath

The rose has been known throughout the ages as a metaphor for devotion, and the symbolism of rose colors is legendary. Red stands for love, white for loyalty, yellow for friendship, light pink for admiration, and dark pink for gratitude.

Contrast the paper-thin petals of a silk or paper rose with the plump spirals in the center of these fanciful felt roses. These handmade blooms have a charm and a quirkiness that can't be mass-produced. After you decorate your house with these whimsical roses, make one to decorate your lapel.

1. From bright pink felt, cut nine shapes with Pattern A, page 39.

2. Fold top of one shape down where indicated and with bright pink thread, whipstitch folded edge down. Repeat on remaining shapes.

3. From green print fabric, cut nine arcs with Pattern B, page 39.

4. From fusible web, cut nine arcs with Pattern C, page 39.

5. Remove backing paper from one fusible web arc. Matching top edges, place one fusible arc, adhesive-side down, on wrong side of one fabric arc. Fuse in place. Repeat for a total of nine arcs, as shown at right.

6. Place one pink felt shape on work surface with folded edge up.

7. Remove backing paper from fused web arcs and place fabric arcs on notched edge of pink felt shape. Overlap ½" to cover notches, as shown below. Fuse in place and repeat for remaining shapes.

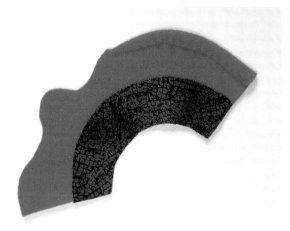

8. Starting at folded side, roll to create rose shape.

9. With green thread, whipstitch edge of green fabric to secure, as shown here.

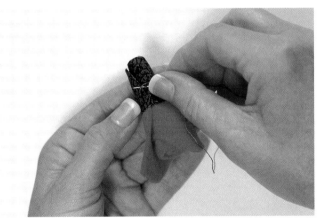

10. With green thread, wrap end, as shown below.

11. Repeat steps 8 through 10 to create remaining roses.

12. To shape flower, fold down top edges of felt indicated on Pattern A and with pink thread, hand stitch in place, as shown below.

13. From wire, cut nine 12" lengths.

14. Fold one wire length in half, and at fold, bend slightly to create small hook.

15. Insert both ends of the folded wire through center of rose and thread through. Hook will hold wire in place.

16. Separate wire ends and wrap around wreath.

17. Repeat steps 14 through 16 for remaining flowers and spacing evenly, wrap around wreath, as shown in Diagram A.

18. Working in small sections, separate moss, and glue moss around roses.

19. Fold twine in half and loop around wreath to hang.

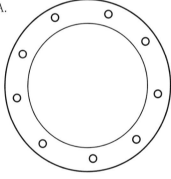

Diagram A

- 5 bright pink felt cuts (9" x 12")
- ¼-yard green print fabric
- ¼-yard fusible web
- Bright pink thread
- Green thread
- 13 feet 18-gauge paper-covered wire stems
- Wire cutters
- Green floral tape
- 1 package dried green Runculus
- 1 package dried green raffia
- 7"-diameter bowl or vase (approximately 5" tall)
- Styrofoam to fit bowl or vase
- Double-sided tape
- Iron

Rose Centerpiece

Felt buds are threaded on paper-wrapped wire to create stemmed roses. Arrange them in a lovely vase or wrap them in tissue to present to someone you love.

1. From bright pink felt, cut nine shapes with Pattern A on facing page.

2. Fold top of one shape down where indicated and with bright pink thread, whipstitch folded edge down. Repeat on remaining shapes.

3. From green print fabric, cut nine arcs with Pattern B, facing page.

4. From fusible web, cut nine arcs with Pattern C, facing page.

5. Remove backing paper from one fusible web arc. Matching top edges, place one fusible arc, adhesive-side down, on wrong side of one fabric arc. Fuse in place. Repeat for a total of nine arcs, as shown in the photo for step 5 of the Rose Wreath project, page 36.

6. Place one pink felt shape on work surface with folded edge up.

7. Remove backing paper from fused web arcs and place fabric arcs on notched edge of pink felt shape. Overlap ½" to cover notches, as shown in the step 7 photo of the Rose Wreath project, page 37. Fuse in place and repeat for remaining shapes.

8. Cut wire into 13 pieces, each 12" long.

9. Thread one wire through the center of one rose.

10. Starting at folded side, roll one felt shape around one wire stem to create rose.

11. With green thread, hand stitch exposed side of green fabric to secure, as shown in the photo for step 9 of the Rose Wreath project, page 37.

12. With green thread wrap bottom of rose around stem to secure.

13. Repeat steps 9 through 12 for remaining 12 roses.

14. To shape flower, fold down top edges of felt indicated on Pattern A and with pink thread, hand stitch in place, as shown in the photo for step 12 of the Rose Wreath project, page 37.

15. Trim Styrofoam to fit inside bowl or vase. It should be 2" lower than lip of bowl or vase.

16. Secure Styrofoam to bowl or vase with double-sided tape.

17. Arrange raffia loosely on top of Styrofoam.

18. With wire cutters, trim roses to desired length and insert stems in Styrofoam as desired.

19. Insert ends of Runculus in Styrofoam around roses as filler.

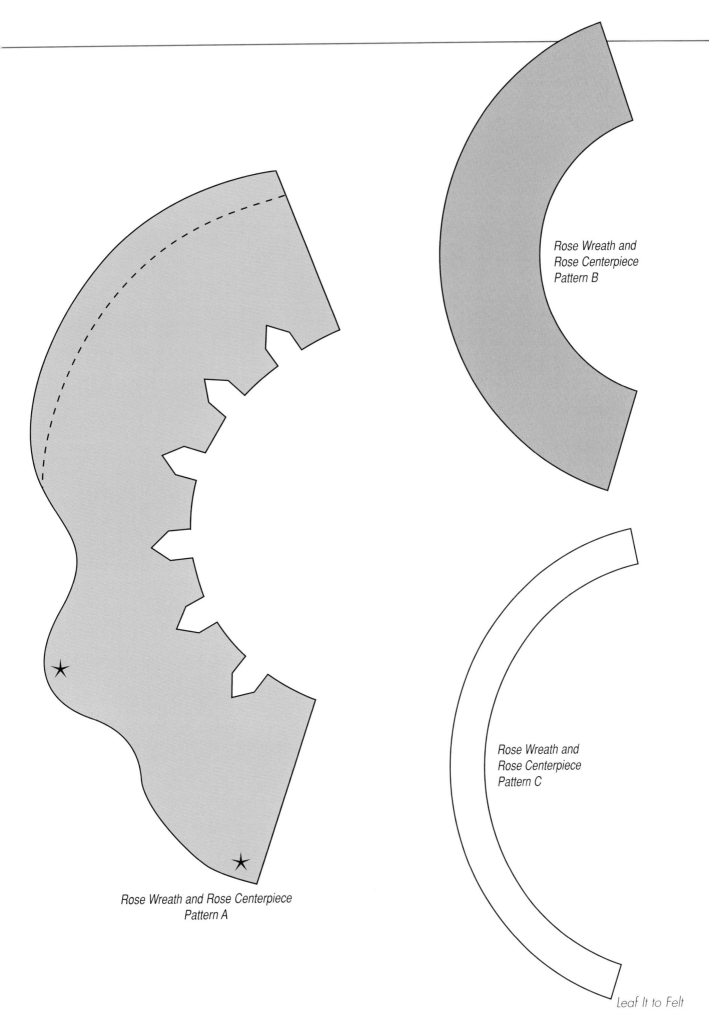

Rose Wreath and
Rose Centerpiece
Pattern B

Rose Wreath and
Rose Centerpiece
Pattern C

Rose Wreath and Rose Centerpiece
Pattern A

❖ ½-yard green felt
❖ ⅓-yard lace fabric
❖ 12-oz. can white spray paint
❖ Green thread
❖ 14" twig (rigid)
❖ 26" twig (bendable)
❖ 1 skein brown embroidery floss
  or small package of twine
❖ 2 blocks 7⅞" x 3⅞" x 2¾" floral foam
❖ Craft knife
❖ Dried flowers
❖ Sewing machine

All seam allowances are ¼".

Green Faux Lace Pocket

The most striking feature of lace is the part that is missing! The negative spaces are formed as the lace is crafted, rather than cut away afterwards. These negative spaces are highlighted with ordinary spray paint to make airy and graceful patterns on felt. The faint lace flowers reproduced on the felt pockets harmonize with the dried flowers perched inside.

1. From green felt, cut two 10½" x 12½" rectangles.

2. From lace fabric, cut one 10½" x 12½" rectangle.

3. In a well-ventilated area, place one green felt rectangle on work surface and then layer the lace rectangle on top of the felt rectangle, as shown below.

4. Hold spray can 10" to 12" from surface and spray evenly over lace, as shown here.

5. Let dry and then remove lace, as shown at right.

6. Right sides together, machine stitch sides and bottom of rectangles together, starting and stopping 4" from tops of sides, as shown in Diagram A.

Diagram A

7. Cut horizontal slit through both layers at 4" from tops of sides, as shown in Diagram B.

Diagram B

8. Fold bottom corners diagonally and machine stitch 2" diagonal seams in corners, as shown in Diagram C.

Diagram C

9. Trim and turn right-side out, as shown at right.

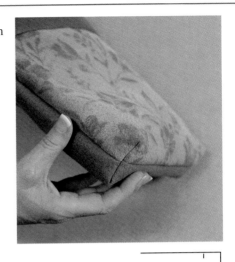

10. Machine stitch 4" lengths of side seams with seams out, as shown in Diagram D.

11. Finger press 4" side seams open and fold down top 1¼" to make cuff. Fold down again 1½" and whipstitch cuff in place, as shown below.

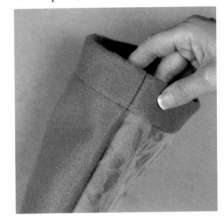

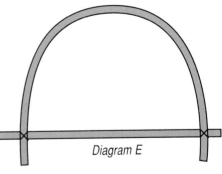

Diagram D

12. Place short twig on work surface. Bend long twig and lash bent twig to short twig at intersection by wrapping both with floss or twine. Knot securely and trim ends, as shown in Diagram E.

Diagram E

13. Whipstitch twigs to back of the pocket.

14. Cut floral foam to fit and then arrange and insert flowers.

Note: When choosing spray paint, do not buy metallic colors. They may damage your sewing machine.

❖ ½-yard gray felt
❖ ⅓-yard lace fabric
❖ 12-oz. can light gray spray paint
❖ Gray thread
❖ 1 skein brown embroidery floss
  or small package twine
❖ 2 blocks 7⅞" x 3⅞" x 2¾" floral foam
❖ 14" twig (rigid)
❖ 26" twig (bendable)
❖ Dried flowers
❖ Sewing machine

All seam allowances are ¼".

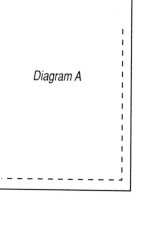

Gray Faux Lace Pocket

Using the same method as in the Green Faux Lace Pocket, this variation in a different color is great if green does not fit into your décor. Though similar, the difference between these two projects is in the cuff. You'll be surprised by how different a change in folding and stitching makes the finished projects look.

1. From gray felt, cut two 10½" x 12½" rectangles.

2. From lace fabric, cut one 10½" x 12½" rectangle.

3. In a well-ventilated area place one gray felt rectangle on work surface and then layer the lace rectangle on top of the felt rectangle, as shown in the photo for step 3 of the Green Faux Lace Pocket, page 40.

4. Hold spray can 10" to 12" from surface and spray evenly over lace, as shown in the step 4 photo of the green pocket project, page 40.

5. Let dry and then remove lace, as shown in the step 5 photo of the green pocket project, page 41.

6. Right sides together, machine stitch sides and bottom of rectangles together starting and stopping 4" from tops of sides, as shown in Diagram A here.

7. Cut horizontal slit through both layers at 4" from tops of sides, as shown in Diagram B.

8. Fold bottom corners diagonally and machine stitch 2" diagonal seams in corners, as shown in Diagram C.

Diagram A

Diagram B

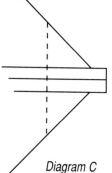

Diagram C

9. Trim and turn right-side out.

10. Fold top down to make cuff and use a running stitch by hand to secure in cuff diagonally following stitched seam, as shown below.

11. Place short twig on work surface. Bend long twig and lash bent twig to short twig at intersection by wrapping both with floss or twine. Knot securely and trim ends, as shown in Diagram E.

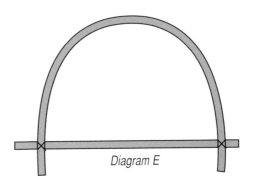

Diagram E

12. Whipstitch twigs to back of pocket.

13. Cut floral foam to fit and then arrange and insert flowers.

chapter four

On a Mission

"**H**ave nothing in your houses that you do not know to be useful or believe to be beautiful." —William Morris As a protest against the ornamentation and mass-production of Victorian furniture, Morris and his contemporaries designed pieces that were characterized by clean lines and natural beauty. This movement came to be known as the Mission Style and later evolved into the Prairie and Arts and Crafts styles. Artists and craftspeople, most of whom worked in the Midwest and in California, made pottery, metalwork, stained glass, textiles, and sculpture, integrating this style into their work.

materials needed

❖ ⅓-yard cobblestone wool felt (20% wool/80% rayon)
❖ 9" x 12" cut blue felt
❖ 9" x 12" cut bronze felt
❖ ⅛-yard orange wool felt
❖ ¼-yard charcoal gray felt
❖ 12" pillow form
❖ Blue thread
❖ Bronze thread
❖ Orange thread
❖ 9" x 12" stencil blank or Mylar sheet
❖ Stencil brush
❖ 2-oz. bottle dark purple acrylic craft paint
❖ Craft knife
❖ Permanent marker
❖ Sewing machine
❖ Iron

All seam allowances are ¼".

Blue Mission Pillow

Inspired by the geometric designs of Frank Lloyd Wright's stained glass windows, this project and the one that follows are meant for Prairie interiors. Some architects and designers from this period, 1880 to 1920, actually borrowed designs from Mayan bas-relief sculpture. In order to mimic the depth and complexity of bas-relief, the centers of these appliqués are stenciled with contrasting colors of smoky purple and brown.

1. Before you begin, refer to General Instructions for Stenciling, page 11.

2. With permanent marker, trace Stencil Pattern A, page 48, on Mylar and cut out.

3. Being sure to allow enough space around each design to cut appliqué shapes from felt, stencil four designs on blue felt, allowing enough space between each stenciled design to cut shapes from felt. Let dry.

4. Center stenciled designs and cut out four shapes with Appliqué Pattern A, page 48.

5. From bronze felt, cut notched border with Pattern B, page 48, turning and completing pattern to make complete square. (Note overlaps.)

6. From cobblestone felt, cut one 10" square for pillow top.

7. Place blue shapes in center of cobblestone felt square, as shown in Diagram A. Pin or baste in place and with blue thread, hand appliqué blue shapes to pillow top. Remove basting stitches if necessary. (Refer to General Instructions for Hand Appliqué, page 10.)

8. Place notched border on felt square, centering blue shapes inside. Pin or baste in place and with bronze thread, hand appliqué border to felt square. Remove basting stitches if necessary.

9. From orange wool fabric, cut four 1¾" x 12½" strips for border.

10. Right sides together, center border strips to sides of felt square and with orange thread, machine stitch strips to felt, starting and stopping seams ¼" from ends. Miter corners. (Refer to General Instructions for Mitered Corners, page 10.) Press.

11. With orange thread, hand stitch running stitch along orange border, ¼" from seam.

12. From charcoal felt, cut one 12½" square for pillow back.

13. Right sides together and with orange thread, machine stitch front to back leaving opening to insert pillow form. Trim excess fabric from corners. (Refer to General Instructions for Trimming Corners, page 10.)

14. Turn right-side out, insert pillow form, and whipstitch opening closed with orange thread

Diagram A

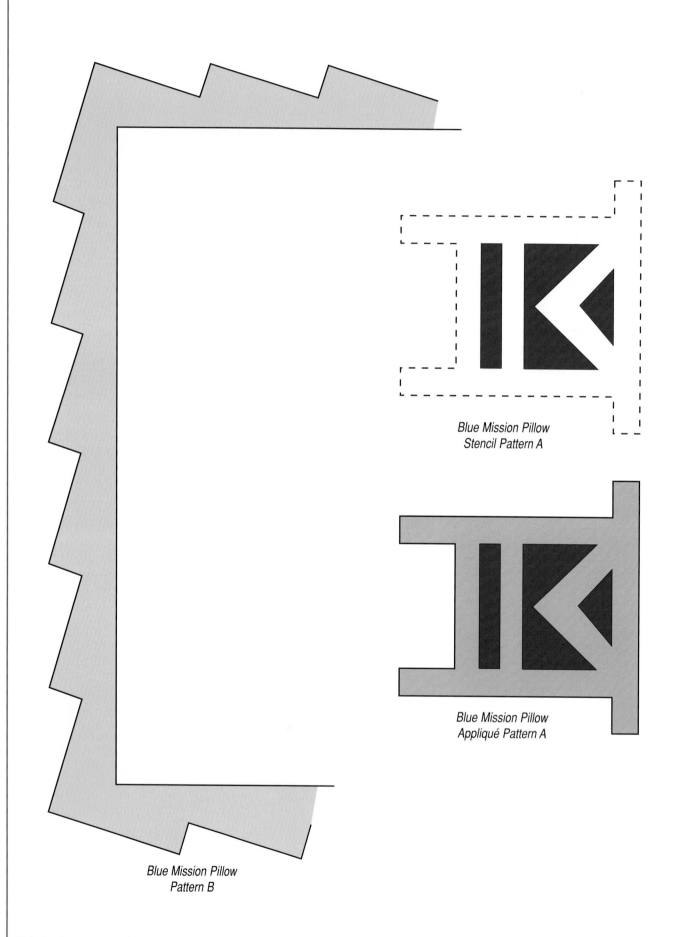

Blue Mission Pillow
Stencil Pattern A

Blue Mission Pillow
Appliqué Pattern A

Blue Mission Pillow
Pattern B

❖ ⅓-yard cobblestone wool felt
   (20% wool/80% rayon)
❖ 9" x 12" cut green felt
❖ ⅛-yard orange wool felt
❖ ¼-yard charcoal gray felt
❖ 12" pillow form
❖ Green thread
❖ Orange thread
❖ 9" x 12" stencil blank or Mylar sheet
❖ Stencil brush
❖ 2-oz. bottle dark brown acrylic craft paint
❖ Craft knife
❖ Permanent marker
❖ Sewing machine
❖ Iron

All seam allowances are ¼".

Green Mission Pillow

Another great piece to display in a Prairie interior, this pillow is a variation of the Blue Mission Pillow. Not only are the colors different, but the geometric stencil designs vary as well—simple changes that create a different look.

1. Before you begin, refer to General Instructions for Stenciling, page 11.

2. With permanent marker, trace Stencil Pattern A, page 50, on Mylar and cut out.

3. Being sure to allow enough space around each design to cut appliqué shapes from felt, stencil four designs on green felt, allowing enough space between each stenciled design to cut shapes from felt. Let dry.

4. Center stenciled designs and cut out four shapes with Appliqué Pattern A, page 50.

5. From cobblestone felt, cut one 10" square for pillow top.

6. Place green shapes in center of felt square, as shown in Diagram A. Pin or baste in place and with green thread, hand appliqué green shapes to pillow top. Remove basting stitches if necessary. (Refer to General Instructions for Hand Appliqué, page 10.)

Diagram A

7. From orange wool fabric, cut four 1¾" x 12½" strips for border.

8. Right sides together, center border strips to sides of felt square and with orange thread, machine stitch strips to felt, starting and stopping seams ¼" from ends. Miter corners. (Refer to General Instructions for Mitered Corners, page 10.) Press.

9. With orange thread, hand stitch running stitch along orange border, ¼" from seam.

10. From charcoal felt, cut one 12½" square for pillow back.

11. Right sides together and with orange thread, machine stitch front to back leaving opening to insert pillow form. Trim excess fabric from corners. (Refer to General Instructions for Trimming Corners, page 10.)

12. Turn right-side out, insert pillow form, and whipstitch opening closed with orange thread.

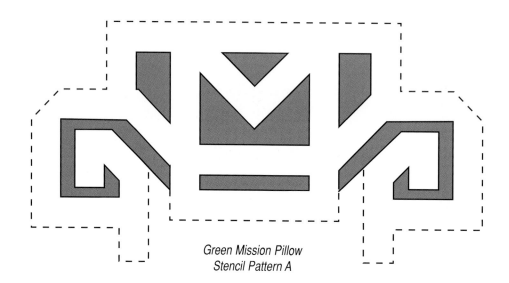

Green Mission Pillow
Stencil Pattern A

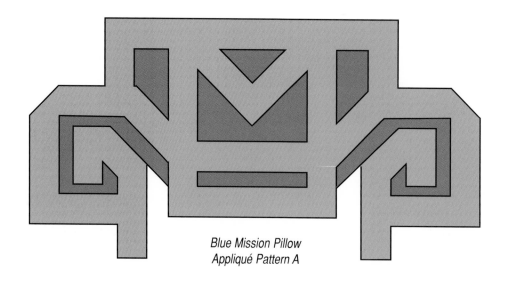

Blue Mission Pillow
Appliqué Pattern A

❖ Fabric-covered photo
  album with window
  (model measures
  14½" x 11½")
❖ ½-yard burgundy felt
❖ 9" x 12" cut blue felt
❖ 9" x 12" cut
  green felt
❖ 9" x 12" cut
  lavender felt
❖ Blue thread
❖ Green thread
❖ Lavender thread
❖ 2 stencil blanks
  or Mylar sheets
  (9" x 12")
❖ Stencil brush
❖ 2-oz. bottle
  dark purple
  acrylic craft paint
❖ Craft knife
❖ Permanent marker
❖ White craft glue
❖ Masking tape

Mission Photo Album

This album duplicates the concept of using geometric designs. Either display the album in the same room along with your pillows, or present it as a gift for that friend or family member who loves the look of a Prairie interior.

1. Before you begin, refer to General Instructions for Stenciling, page 11.

2. With permanent marker, trace Stencil Pattern A, page 53, on Mylar and cut out.

3. Being sure to allow enough space around each design to cut appliqué shapes from felt, stencil one design on lavender felt. Let dry.

4. Reverse stencil pattern to create mirror image and stencil again on lavender felt. Let dry.

5. Stencil one design on green felt. Let dry.

6. Reverse stencil pattern to create mirror image and stencil again on green felt.

7. With permanent marker, trace Stencil Pattern B, page 53, on Mylar and cut out.

8. Stencil two Pattern B designs on blue felt. Let dry.

9. With permanent marker, trace Stencil Pattern C, page 53, on Mylar and cut out.

10. Stencil one design on green felt. Let dry.

11. Stencil one design on blue felt. Let dry.

12. Center stenciled designs on corresponding appliqué patterns on page 54 and cut out shapes. Cut "legs" from Pattern C stenciled on blue felt. Refer to project photo for guidance.

13. From burgundy felt, cut one 17½" x 14½" rectangle to cover album front. (1½" is added to all sides to allow for finishing edges. Make adjustments to your album, if necessary.)

14. Mark placement for window. Place shapes on rectangle, as shown in Diagram A. Pin or baste in place and with matching thread, hand appliqué shapes to album cover. (See General Instructions for Hand Appliqué, page 10.) Remove basting stitches if necessary.

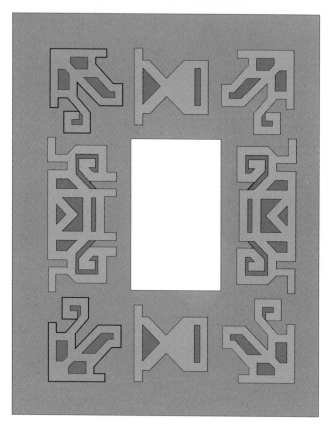

Diagram A

15. Remove album front from center pages and album back.

16. Cut window in felt to match window on album.

17. Apply thin layer of craft glue on album around widow and outside edge of album. Matching windows, place felt on album and carefully smooth into place. Let dry.

18. Cut corners of felt, as shown in Diagram B.

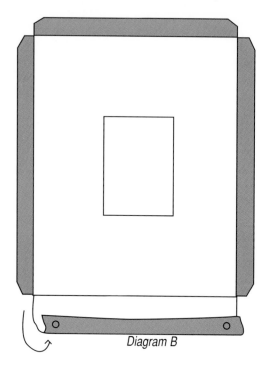

Diagram B

19. Apply thin layer of craft glue 1" around outside edge of reverse side of album front. Wrap edges of felt from front to reverse side and carefully smooth into place. Let dry.

20. Measure inside window of album. From black mat board, cut ⅜"-wide border with inside measurement matching inside measurement of album window. To cut mat board, see steps 1 and 2 from the instructions for the Yo-Yo Frame, page 98.

21. Apply thin layer of glue to back of border. Match to window of album and glue in place.

22. Attach photo to reverse side of front cover, secure in place, and reassemble album

Note: If you want the black mat board border to appear inset in felt, trim felt to match outside edge of border before gluing in place.

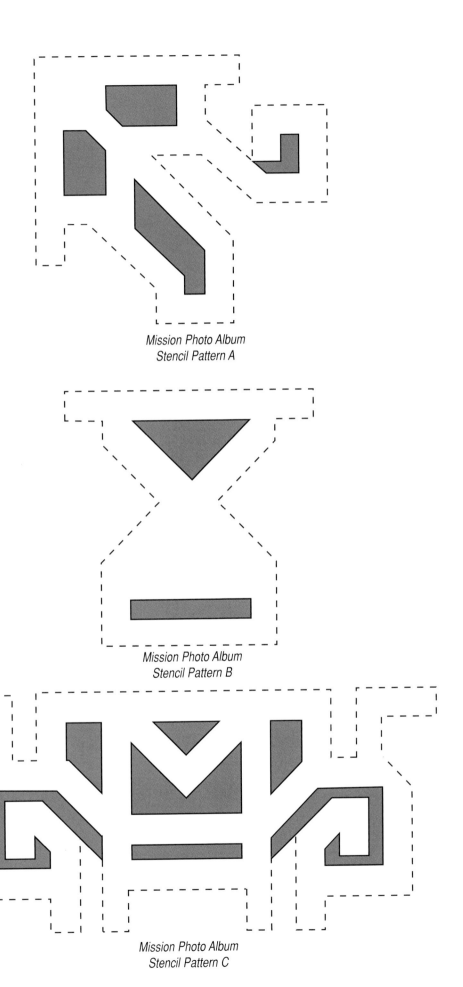

Mission Photo Album
Stencil Pattern A

Mission Photo Album
Stencil Pattern B

Mission Photo Album
Stencil Pattern C

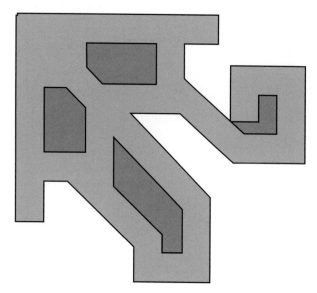

Mission Photo Album
Appliqué Pattern A

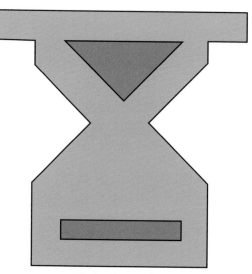

Mission Photo Album
Appliqué Pattern B

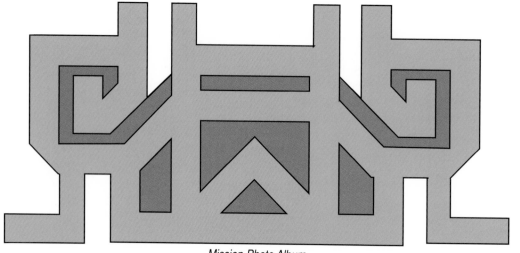

Mission Photo Album
Appliqué Pattern C

- 12½ yards ³⁄₁₆" cotton cord (amount may vary depending on size of basket)
- Basket (model measures 8½" in diameter and 6" tall)
- Scraps of felt in the following colors: ivory, cream, pale yellow, and tan (at least ³⁄₈" wide and 6" to 11" long).
- Small skeins or scrap lengths of acrylic yarn in the following colors: cream, tan, mint green, olive green, and sage green
- Hot glue gun and glue sticks

Covered Cord Basket

Fiber artists are able to make large-scale, dimensional pieces by covering convex surfaces with cord or bundled threads. Disguise run of the mill cotton cord with colorful felt and yarn, and then transform ordinary objects such as baskets or Styrofoam balls. This dressed-up cord is also malleable enough to turn and twist on a flat surface for embellishment.

1. Cut felt into ³⁄₈"-wide strips between 6" and 11" in length. The total number of strips needed will depend on the size and shape of your basket, as well as how long you cut each strip and how tightly the strips are wrapped.

2. To begin, wrap one strip of felt over end of cord as shown in the photo at right and glue in place.

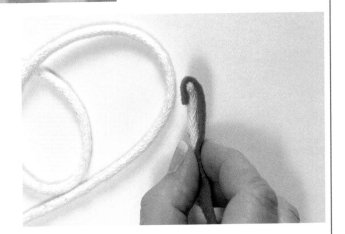

3. Working left to right, continue wrapping felt strip around cord, leaving approximately ⅛" between wraps, as shown here. Glue end of first felt strip to cord.

4. Change color and abut end of new strip to previous strip. Glue in place and continue wrapping diagonally as shown below and then glue end of felt strip to cord.

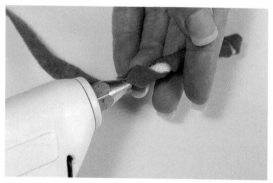

5. After wrapping and gluing a few strips of felt in place, return to beginning point on cord and cut 8" to 12" lengths of two colors of yarn.

6. Hold ends of yarn together and glue to cord in space between felt, as shown.

7. Wrap yarn diagonally in spaces between felt as shown below and glue ends of yarn to cord.

8. Change colors of yarn and slightly overlap ends of new yarn lengths to previous lengths. Glue in place and trim excess yarn where overlap occurs.

9. Working in sections, wrap cord with felt and then with yarn until desired length is covered.

10. To cover ends, cut cord ½" shorter than felt. Wrap felt around cord end and hand stitch in place.

11. Glue covered cord to basket beginning at basket top. Slightly angle end of cord downward so it will tuck under following row, as shown below. Continue gluing until basket is covered. Tuck opposite end under previous row.

Note: If entire length of cord is too unwieldy to cover, cut cord into smaller, more manageable lengths.

❖ 3½ yards cotton cord
❖ 2½" Styrofoam ball
❖ Scraps of felt in the following
  colors: purple, bronze, brown,
  gray/blue, dark red, and
  turquoise (at least ⅜" wide
  and 3" to 6" long).
❖ Small skeins or scrap
  lengths of acrylic yarn in the
  following colors: rust, cream,
  light blue, and yellow
❖ Hot glue gun and glue sticks

Covered Cord Ball

*Colorful and fun, this
ball is created similarly to
the Covered Cord Basket
and can be duplicated in
different colors for use as a
small decorative accent
anywhere in your home.*

1. Cut felt into ⅜" wide strips between 3" and 6" in length.
The total number of strips needed will depend on how
long you cut each strip and how tightly the strips are
wrapped.

2. Follow steps 2 through 10 of the Covered Cord Basket
project, pages 55 and 56, to cover cord.

3. Tightly coil cord to begin, and glue to Styrofoam ball.
Cover entire ball. Coil at end and glue in place, as shown in
the photo at right.

- ❖ 3½ yards cotton cord
- ❖ 2½" Styrofoam ball
- ❖ Scraps of felt in the following colors: cream, tan, lavender, gold, gray, gray/blue, and bronze (at least ⅜" wide and 3" to 6" long).
- ❖ Small skeins or scrap lengths of acrylic yarn in the following colors: rust, light blue, and yellow
- ❖ Hot glue gun and glue sticks
- ❖ Floss covered bead
- ❖ Tassel
- ❖ 1 yard tan rayon cord
- ❖ 6 small metal rings

Covered Cord Ornament

This is a hanging variation of the Covered Cord Ball that will look great on your Christmas tree. And, it's easy enough to make for those traditional ornament exchanges with family and friends.

1. Cut felt into ⅜" wide strips between 3" and 6" in length. The total number of strips needed will depend on how long you cut each strip and how tightly the strips are wrapped.

2. Follow steps 2 through 10 of the Covered Cord Basket project, pages 55 and 56, to cover cord.

3. Cut one 12" length of rayon cord, fold in half, and thread looped end 4½" through floss-covered bead.

4. Glue bead to Styrofoam ball and glue tassel to opposite end of ball.

5. Tuck end of covered cord under bead and glue covered cord to ball. Wrap end of covered cord around tassel.

6. Thread one metal ring on looped rayon cord and tie knot next to ring. Thread rings on ends of rayon cord and knot.

7. Cut two 12" lengths of rayon cord, wrap each around tassel at center, and knot.

8. Thread remaining rings on ends of rayon cord and knot.

- ❖ 7 yards cotton cord
- ❖ Scraps of felt in the following colors: taupe, sage green, teal, blue, cream, burgundy, and gold (at least ⅜" wide and 6" to 8" long).
- ❖ Small skeins or scrap lengths of acrylic yarn in the following colors: mint green, blue, purple, and cream
- ❖ Hot glue gun and glue sticks
- ❖ ¾-yard purple felt
- ❖ ½-yard rust textured fabric
- ❖ ¾-yard purple print cotton fabric
- ❖ Purple thread
- ❖ Sewing machine
- ❖ Iron

All seam allowances are ¼".

Covered Cord Table Runner

This meandering cord looks fabulous on both ends of this contemporary accent piece.

1. Cut one 3½-yard length of cotton cord and cut felt into ⅜"-wide strips between 6" and 8" in length. The total number of strips needed will depend on how long you cut each strip and how tightly the strips are wrapped.

2. Follow steps 2 through 10 of the Covered Cord Basket project, pages 55 and 56, to cover cord.

3. Repeat for remaining 3½-yard length of cotton cord.

4. From purple felt, cut two 11" x 22½" rectangles for runner top.

5. Machine stitch short sides together to make one 11" x 44½" rectangle and press.

6. From textured fabric, cut two 11" x 13½" rectangles.

7. Machine stitch short sides to opposite ends of felt rectangle and press.

8. From purple print fabric, cut two 11" x 35½" rectangles for runner back.

9. Machine stitch short sides together to make one 11" x 70½" rectangle and press.

10. Right sides together, machine stitch runner top to runner back, leaving 6" opening for turning. Trim excess fabric from corners. (Refer to General Instructions for Trimming Corners, page 10.)

11. Turn right-side out, whipstitch opening closed, and press.

12. Using Diagram A as a guide, arrange one length of covered cord on textured fabric. Stitching through all layers, whipstitch in place. Repeat for opposite end of table runner.

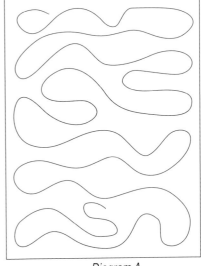

Diagram A

chapter five

You've Been Framed

Photo frames come in a close second to throw pillows for the most popular decorating accessory. Use felt to adorn inexpensive wood frames or make your own frames with foam board. Then pop in photos of family, friends, pets, or even your prize-winning petunias.

❖ 4⅜" x 6⅛"
   rectangle Foam Core
❖ 9" x 12" cuts of felt in the
   following colors: medium blue,
   light blue, gold, fuchsia,
   cream, turquoise, and
   lime green
❖ 4" x 4" scrap
   turquoise print fabric
❖ 2½" x 3⅛"
   rectangle chipboard
❖ Craft knife
❖ White craft glue
❖ 3 3mm turquoise beads
❖ Thread in the following colors:
   light blue, gold, fuchsia,
   cream, turquoise, and
   lime green
❖ 2-oz. bottle lavender
   acrylic craft paint
❖ Wrong end of paintbrush
   (³⁄₁₆" in diameter)

Gable Appliquéd Frame

A basic architectural shape, the gable is a simple triangle that crowns a window or a door. This dressed-up frame is topped with a bright, flowery gable and accented with splashy patterns of dots and waves.

1. With craft knife, cut one Pattern A shape, page 64, from Foam Core.

2. From medium blue felt, cut one Pattern B shape, page 65, for frame front.

3. Referring to Pattern B, page 65, cut appliqué shapes from corresponding felt colors.

4. Pin or baste felt pieces in place and with matching colors of thread, hand appliqué shapes in place.

(See General Instructions for Hand Appliqué, page 10.) Remove basting stitches if necessary.

5. With turquoise thread, hand stitch beads to flower centers as indicated on Pattern B.

6. Place frame front right-side down on work surface. Matching outside edges, place Pattern A Foam Core shape on wrong side of frame front. Apply thin layer of craft glue approximately ½" wide around window of Foam Core.

7. Wrap felt flaps through window and glue in place. Let dry.

8. From cream felt, cut one ⅜" x 19" strip for frame edge.

9. With cream thread, whipstitch frame edge to frame front, as shown below.

10. From gold felt, cut one Pattern A shape, page 64, for frame back.

11. With cream thread, whipstitch frame back to frame edge.

12. With gold thread, whipstitch frame back to blue felt around inside of window.

13. With craft knife, cut one Pattern C, page 64, from chipboard.

14. From turquoise print fabric, cut one Pattern D shape, page 65.

15. Place Pattern D shape right-side down on work surface. Apply thin coat of craft glue to chipboard front. Center and glue to Pattern D shape. Let dry.

16. Apply thin coat of craft glue to chipboard back. Wrap excess turquoise fabric to chipboard back and glue in place. Let dry.

17. Apply craft glue to wrong side of covered chipboard, center on frame front and glue in place. Let dry.

18. To make dots, dip wrong end of paintbrush in paint and press on wave shapes and small circles as indicated in the photo below. Let dry.

19. Insert photo and secure in place.

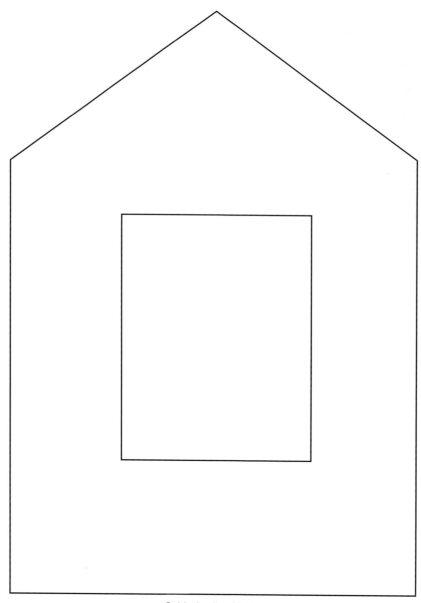

*Gable Appliquéd Frame
Pattern A*

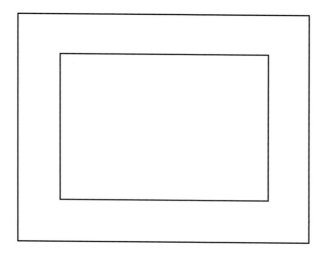

*Gable Appliquéd Frame
Pattern C*

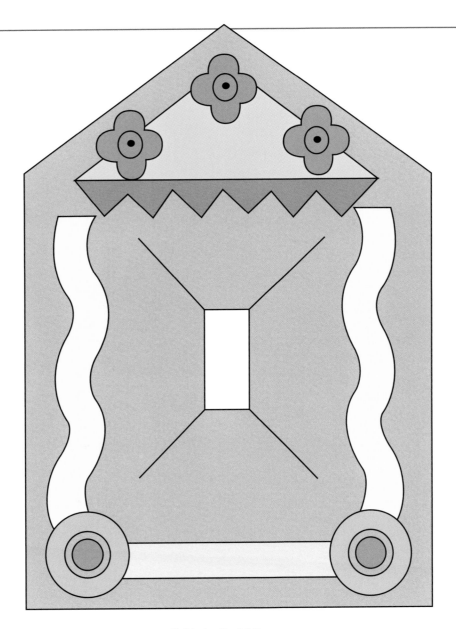

Gable Appliquéd Frame
Pattern B

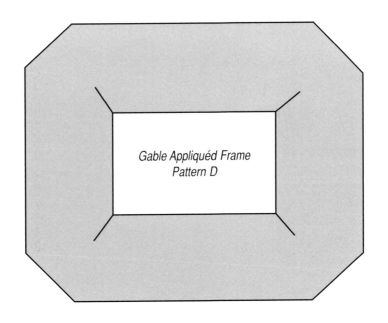

Gable Appliquéd Frame
Pattern D

❖ 4⅞" x 6⅛"
   rectangle Foam Core
❖ 9" x 12" cuts of felt in the
   following colors: dark blue,
   dark green, purple, violet,
   fuchsia, and brown
❖ 5" x 6" scrap
   blue cotton fabric
❖ 2⅞" x 4" rectangle chipboard
❖ Craft knife
❖ White craft glue
❖ 12 3mm blue beads
❖ 1 package
   4mm dusty pink silk ribbon
❖ Thread in the following
   colors: dark green, purple,
   violet, fuchsia, and brown
❖ Pink embroidery floss
❖ Iron

Floral Appliquéd Frame

A favorite technique of designers is to combine different colors of similar values—the value being the degree of light or dark of an individual hue. The collection of dark hues, and the curve of the outer edge, make this frame interesting and attractive.

1. With craft knife, cut one Pattern A shape, page 68, from Foam Core.

2. From medium blue felt, cut one Pattern B shape, page 69, for frame front.

3. Referring to Pattern B, page 69, cut appliqué shapes from corresponding felt colors.

4. Pin or baste felt pieces in place and with matching colors of thread, hand appliqué shapes in place. (See General Instructions for Hand Appliqué, page 10.) Remove basting stitches if necessary.

5. With blue thread, hand stitch beads to centers of fuchsia circles as indicated in the photos below.

6. With two strands of pink embroidery floss, stitch centers of purple circles with star stitch, as indicated at right. (Refer to General Instructions for Embroidery Stitches, page 9.)

7. Place frame front right-side down on work surface. Matching outside edges, place Pattern A Foam Core shape on wrong side of frame front. Apply thin layer of craft glue approximately ½" wide around window of Foam Core.

8. Wrap felt flaps through window and glue in place. Let dry.

9. From brown felt, cut one ⅜" x 22" strip for frame edge.

10. With brown thread, whipstitch frame edge to frame front, as shown at right.

11. From green felt, cut one Pattern A shape, page 68, for frame back.

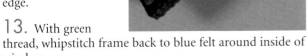

12. With brown thread, whipstitch frame back to frame edge.

13. With green thread, whipstitch frame back to blue felt around inside of window.

14. With craft knife, cut one Pattern C, page 68, from chipboard.

15. From blue fabric, cut one Pattern D shape, page 69.

16. Place Pattern D shape on work surface. Apply thin coat of craft glue to chipboard front. Center and glue to Pattern D shape. Let dry.

17. Apply thin coat of craft glue to chipboard back. Wrap excess blue fabric to chipboard back and glue in place. Let dry.

18. Press ribbon and then glue end to bottom corner of wrong side of wrapped chipboard, as shown in Diagram B. Let dry.

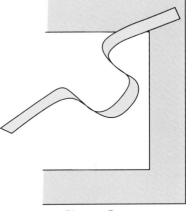

Diagram B

19. Wrap ribbon diagonally six times and trim and glue end to wrong side of wrapped chipboard, as shown in Diagram C. Let dry.

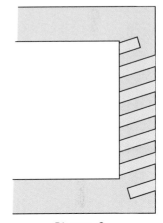

Diagram C

20. Repeat ribbon wrapping for sides, wrapping nine times, and top, wrapping six times, as shown at right.

21. Apply craft glue to wrong side of covered chipboard, center on frame front and glue in place. Let dry.

22. Insert photo and secure in place.

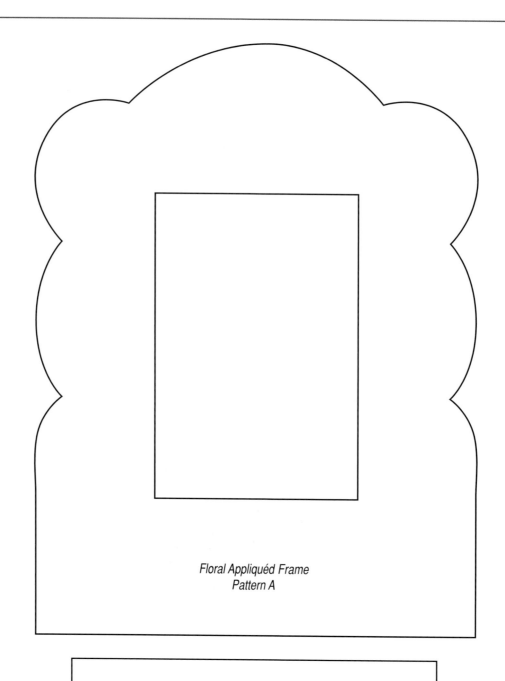

*Floral Appliquéd Frame
Pattern A*

*Floral Appliquéd Frame
Pattern C*

Floral Appliquéd Frame
Pattern B

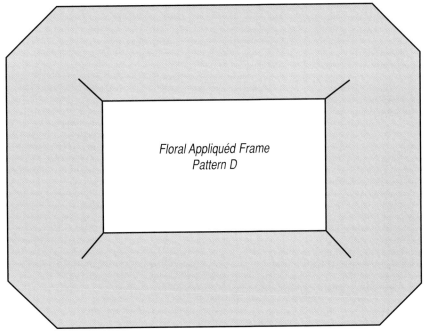

Floral Appliquéd Frame
Pattern D

❖ 5¾" x 6⅞"
  rectangle Foam Core
❖ 9" x 12" cuts of felt in the
  following colors: cream,
  light blue, medium green,
  dark green, purple, fuchsia,
  and gold
❖ 4" x 5" scrap
  fuchsia cotton fabric
❖ 2½" x 3⅜"
  rectangle chipboard
❖ Craft knife
❖ White craft glue
❖ 30 3mm blue beads
❖ 1 package
  4mm light blue silk ribbon
❖ Thread in the following
  colors: light blue, medium
  green, dark green, purple,
  fuchsia, and gold
❖ Iron

Vine Appliquéd Frame

This frame highlights the color range and versatility of felt. It can be cut to form basic geometric shapes, such as squares and rectangles, or it can be snipped to create meandering vines and flower petals. Since cut felt has a clean edge, it is the perfect decorating medium.

1. With craft knife, cut one Pattern A shape, page 72, from Foam Core.

2. From cream felt, cut one Pattern B shape, page 73, for frame front.

3. Referring to Pattern B, page 73, cut appliqué shapes from corresponding felt colors.

4. Pin or baste felt pieces in place and with matching colors of thread, hand appliqué shapes in place. (See General Instructions for Hand Appliqué, page 10.) Remove basting stitches if necessary.

5. With blue thread, hand stitch beads, as shown here.

6. Place frame front right-side down on work surface. Matching outside edges, place Pattern A Foam Core shape on wrong side of frame front. Apply thin layer of craft glue approximately ½" wide around window of Foam Core.

7. Wrap felt flaps through window and glue in place. Let dry.

8. From gold felt, cut one ⅜" x 23" strip for frame edge.

9. With gold thread, whipstitch frame edge to frame front, as shown below.

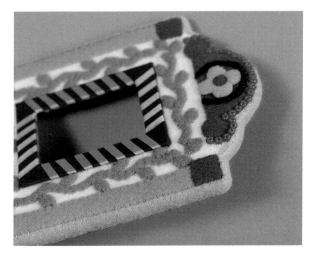

10. From green felt, cut one Pattern A shape for frame back.

11. With gold thread, whipstitch frame back to frame edge.

12. With green thread, whipstitch frame back to cream felt around inside of window.

13. With craft knife, cut one Pattern C, page 72, from chipboard.

14. From fuchsia fabric, cut one Pattern D shape, page 73.

15. Place Pattern D shape on work surface. Apply thin coat of craft glue to chipboard front. Center and glue to Pattern D shape. Let dry.

16. Apply thin coat of craft glue to chipboard back. Wrap excess fuchsia fabric to chipboard back and glue in place. Let dry.

17. Press ribbon. Glue end to bottom corner of wrong side of wrapped chipboard, as shown in Diagram B. Let dry.

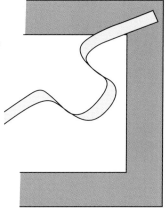

Diagram B

18. Wrap ribbon diagonally five times and trim and glue end to wrong side of wrapped chipboard, as shown in Diagram C at right. Let dry.

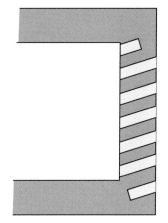

Diagram C

19. Repeat ribbon wrapping for sides, wrapping seven times, and wrapping five times for the top, as shown at right.

20. Apply craft glue to wrong side of covered chipboard, center on frame front, and glue in place. Let dry.

21. Insert photo and secure in place.

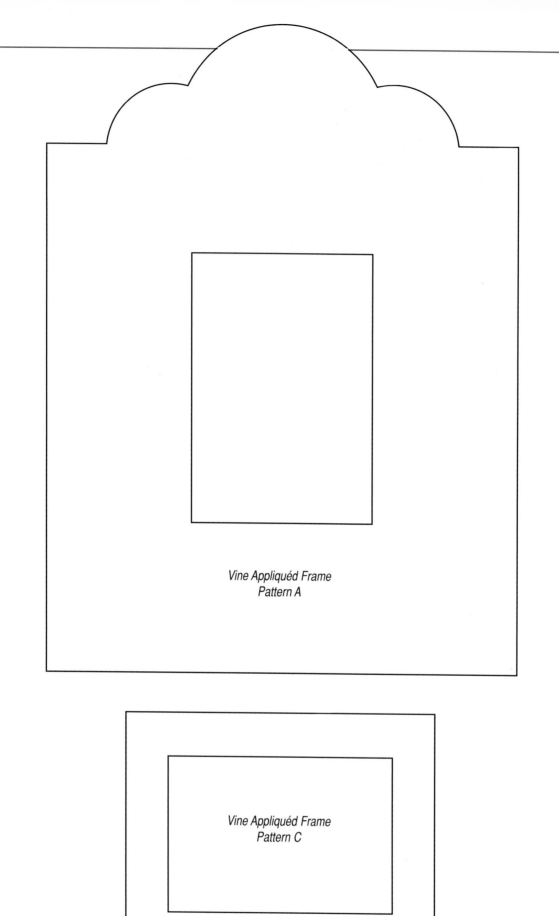

Vine Appliquéd Frame
Pattern A

Vine Appliquéd Frame
Pattern C

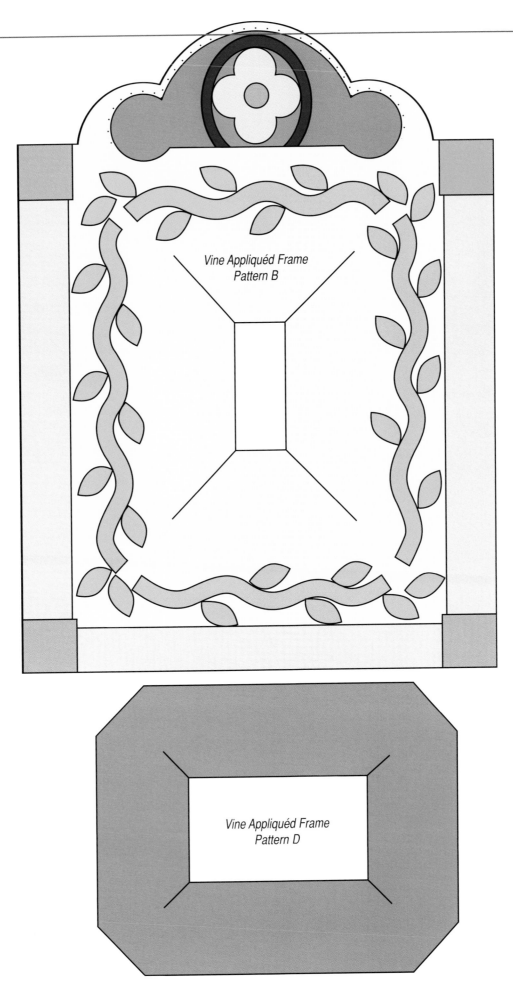

Vine Appliquéd Frame
Pattern B

Vine Appliquéd Frame
Pattern D

materials needed

❖ Frame with recessed mat (model measures 6⅝" square with a 3" square window)
❖ 2 cuts lavender felt (each 9" x 12")
❖ 2 cuts turquoise felt (each 9" x 12")
❖ 2 cuts black felt (each 9" x 12")
❖ 2 cuts brown felt (each 9" x 12")
❖ 9" x 12" cut periwinkle blue felt
❖ 9" x 12" cut ivory felt
❖ Lavender thread
❖ White craft glue

Spiral and Leaf Coiled Frame

This is my favorite felt technique. As each small section must be rolled by hand and secured, it is best to use this technique to cover small areas. Frames, sachets, and mini pillows serve as good surfaces to embellish and the technique works best when using soft felt with more "loft." Allow a few test strips and a few minutes of practice for making shapes. The right tension and size is important, as is the width of the strips. When the shapes are glued in place, the covered area becomes a rich and velvety felt tapestry.

1. Cut felt scraps into ⁵⁄₁₆" x 5" strips for the spirals. When cutting strips in each color, consider that the dominant colors in the model project are lavender and turquoise, followed by brown and black. Use only a slight amount of ivory and periwinkle blue for accents.

2. To make single-color spirals, use one or two strips of the same felt color. To make two-toned spiral, stack two felt strips of contrasting colors, as shown at right.

3. Tightly roll felt into a spiral that is between ⅜" and ⅝" in diameter, as shown below.

4. Trim end and stitch to side of spiral, as shown below.

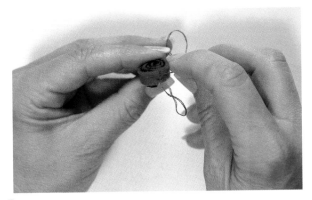

5. Insert needle through sides of spiral several times to secure, as shown at right. Knot end of thread.

6. Cut felt into ⁵⁄₁₆" x 5" strips for the leaves. Again, consider your color scheme as suggested in step 1 when cutting your leaf strips.

7. To make single-color leaves, use one or two strips of the same felt color. To make two-toned leaves, stack two felt strips of contrasting colors, as shown at right.

8. Fold felt strips back and forth, accordion-style. Insert needle through side to secure, as shown here.

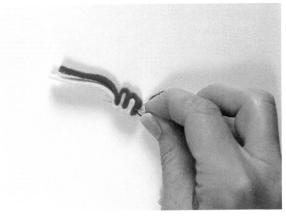

9. Trim ends of felt strips to meet at bottom of shape until they become between ½" and ¾" in diameter and stitch together, as shown below.

10. Make enough spirals and leaves to cover exposed surface of mat. The model project shown here contains approximately 120 individual spirals and leaves.

11. Insert mat in frame and secure.

12. Apply thin coat of craft glue to mat and place spirals and leaves together snugly. Glue in place. Let dry.

13. Insert photo and secure in place.

Note: In order for spirals and leaves to hold their shape, they must be tightly held together. Practice making a few shapes to achieve desired density of felt.

❖ Light wood frame with flat surface (model measures 6¾" x 8¾" with 4" x 6" window)
❖ 9" x 12" cuts of felt in the following colors: purple, orange, cream and lavender
❖ Cream thread
❖ Orange thread
❖ Cream buttons in assorted sizes ⅜" to ½"
❖ White craft glue

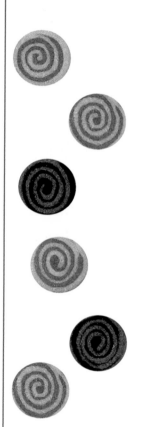

Button and Pinwheel Coiled Frame

This frame, like the Spiral and Leaf Coiled Frame project, features coiled felt strips. Buttons are added for surface texture.

1. Cut felt scraps into ⁵⁄₁₆" x 5" strips for the spirals. You will need 17 strips each from cream and orange felt to complete 17 cream/orange spirals at ¾" to ⅞" in diameter; 12 strips each of orange and purple felt to complete 12 orange/purple spirals at ¾" to ⅞" in diameter; and three strips each of orange and lavender felt to complete three orange/lavender spirals at ¾" to ⅞" in diameter.

2. To make single-color spirals, use one or two strips of the same felt color. To make two-toned spiral, stack two felt strips of contrasting colors, as shown here.

3. Tightly roll felt into a spiral that is between ¾" and ⅞" in diameter.

4. Trim end and stitch to side of spiral, as shown.

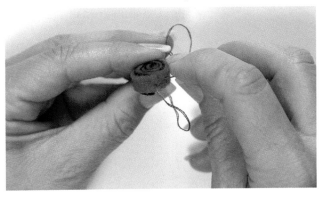

5. Insert needle through sides of spiral several times to secure, as shown. Knot end of thread.

6. Apply thin coat of glue on back of each spiral and glue in place to frame front in random pattern. Refer to project photo if guidance for spiral placement is necessary.

7. Glue buttons to frame front between spirals as desired, leaving exposed areas of wood.

8. Insert photo and secure in place.

chapter six

Have a Ball

The tactile nature of these decorative balls invites you to pick them up and examine them. Many cultures adorn their homes with these non-utilitarian ornaments. The Japanese have been making thread-covered Temari balls for centuries, and the Venetians make most anything out of glass including small reflective globes. This collection has many different textures and surface treatments. They can be grouped in a bowl or on a tray and are meant to be picked up and studied by curious visitors.

❖ 2¾" Styrofoam ball
❖ 9" x 12" cut dusty rose felt
❖ 9" x 12" cut dark green felt
❖ 9" x 12" cut antique gold felt
❖ 9" x 12" cut butterscotch felt
❖ 9" x 12" cut cream felt
❖ Dusty rose thread
❖ White craft glue
❖ 1½ yards gray chenille cord

Rosebud Ball

This small dimensional ball is covered with roses and soft chenille cord. You can use it to decorate a Victorian dresser top or a Victorian Christmas tree.

1. Cut Pattern A shapes as follows:
   ❖ nine from gold felt
   ❖ four from butterscotch felt
   ❖ seven from cream felt
2. From dusty rose felt, cut one ⅜" x 5" strip.

3. Following the five photos in progression below, carefully tie the dusty rose felt strip in single knot, trim ends, and with rose thread, hand tack in place at back of knot to form rose bud. Repeat to make 20 rosebuds.

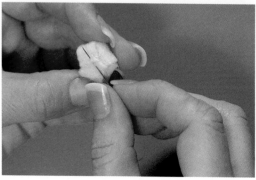

4. From green felt, cut 20 leaf shapes with Pattern B.

5. Place one leaf shape in center of each Pattern A triangle and with rose thread, hand stitch rosebud and leaf shape to center of each triangle.

6. Apply thin layer of glue to backs of the layered triangles and glue these to the ball in random color pattern leaving approximately ⅛" between each triangle. Let dry.

7. Starting at one end of ball—the "North Pole"— cut three 1¾" lengths and one 3½" length of cord.

8. Covering seams, glue cord in place, as shown in Diagram A. Trim ends if necessary.

9. Cut one 8¾" length of cord.

10. Covering seams, glue cord in place, as shown in Diagram B. Trim ends if necessary.

11. Repeat steps 7 through 10 for "South Pole."

12. Cut one 18" length of cord.

13. Glue cord in place, covering remaining seams around center of ball, as shown in Diagram C. Trim if necessary.

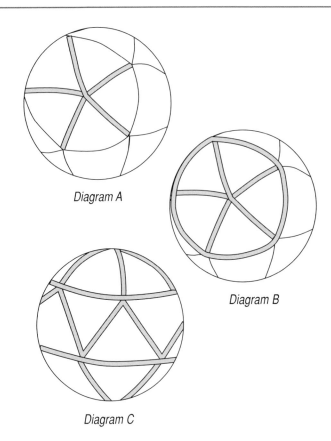

Diagram A

Diagram B

Diagram C

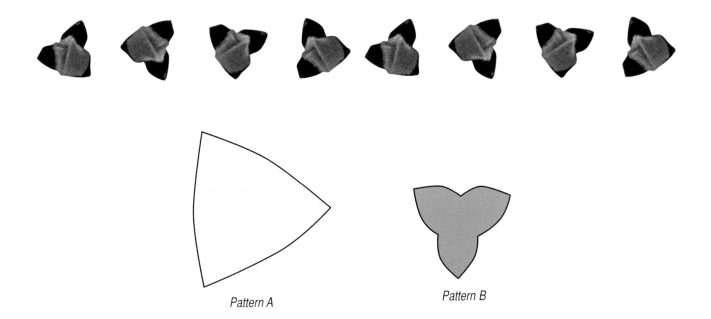

Pattern A

Pattern B

❖ 3¾" Styrofoam ball
❖ 9" x 12" cut
  butterscotch felt
❖ Cream thread

Plain Ball

A simple covered ball crisscrossed with diagonal ribs. The ribs are formed by whipstitching cut edges together.

1. From felt, cut 20 Pattern A shapes.

2. Whipstitch five triangles together to make one pieced section, as shown in Diagram A.

3. Whipstitch five more triangles to the first five triangles, as shown in Diagram B.

4. Repeat steps 2 and 3 to make a second pieced section. Both pieced sections should have 10 triangles each.

5. Wrap pieced sections around ball and whipstitch together, as shown in Diagram C.

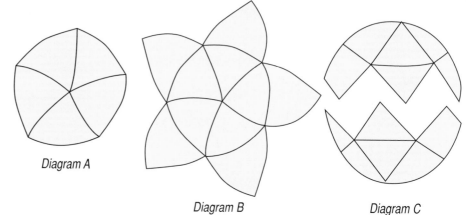

Diagram A

Diagram B

Diagram C

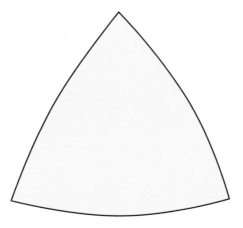

Pattern A

❖ 3¾" Styrofoam ball
❖ 9" x 12" cut cream felt
❖ Scraps of the following colors of felt: light blue, turquoise, antique gold, and lavender
❖ Cream thread
❖ 9" x 12" rectangle water-soluble stabilizer (such as Solvy)
❖ Sewing machine

Confetti Ball

This project is a plain felt ball adorned with tactile felt confetti and serpentine machine stitching. It is a fun and fascinating centerpiece or party favor.

1. From felt scraps, cut small bits, as shown.

2. Arrange bits in desired pattern on cream felt.

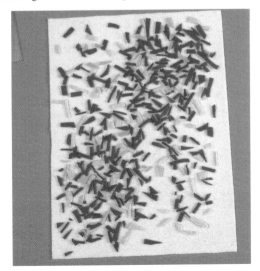

3. Place stabilizer on felt and pin in place.

4. With one continuous seam, machine stitch in random curve pattern. Make enough passes back and forth on the square to secure all bits.

5. Following manufacturer's directions, remove stabilizer by submerging felt in water. Let dry.

6. From dried felt piece, cut 20 Pattern A shapes, facing page.

7. Whipstitch five triangles together to make one pieced section, as shown in Diagram A on facing page.

8. Whipstitch five more triangles to the first five triangles, as shown in Diagram B on facing page.

9. Repeat steps 7 and 8 to make a second pieced section. Both pieced sections should have 10 triangles each.

10. Wrap pieced sections around ball and whipstitch together, as shown in Diagram C on facing page.

❖ 3¾" Styrofoam ball
❖ 9" x 12" cut cream felt
❖ 9" x 12" cut tan felt
❖ 9" x 12" cut cobblestone wool felt (20% wool/80% rayon)
❖ 9" x 12" cut purple felt
❖ 40 buttons in assorted colors and sizes (between ⅜" and ⁹⁄₁₆" wide)
❖ Cream embroidery floss

Button Ball

Need a great way to show off your antique button collection? Display this ball on a shelf with your favorite old marbles or metal lunchbox.

1. Cut Pattern A as follows:
   ❖ Seven from cobblestone felt
   ❖ Seven from cream felt
   ❖ Six from tan felt

2. From all colors of felt, including purple, cut 20 circles with Pattern B and 20 circles with Pattern C.

Diagram A

3. Layer one small circle on one large circle of a contrasting color as indicated in Diagram A, stitch together as in Diagram B, and then stitch to a felt triangle A-shape as in Diagram C. Repeat for a total of 20 triangles.

Diagram B

4. Stitch buttons to triangles, as shown in Diagram C. If desired, cut and layer felt circles under selected buttons before stitching to triangles.

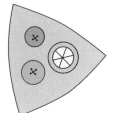

Diagram C

5. Whipstitch five decorated triangles together to make one pieced section, as shown in Diagram D.

Diagram D

6. Whipstitch five more decorated triangles to the first five triangles, as shown in Diagram E.

7. Repeat steps 5 and 6 to make a second pieced section. Both pieced sections should have 10 triangles each.

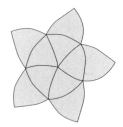

Diagram E

8. Wrap pieced sections around ball and whipstitch together, as shown in Diagram F.

Diagram F

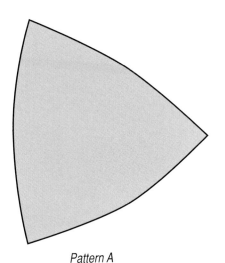

Pattern A

Pattern B

Pattern C

❖ 3¾" Styrofoam ball
❖ 9" x 12" cut
  medium blue felt
❖ 9" x 12" cut
  light blue felt
❖ 9" x 12" cut
  cream felt
❖ Light green floss
❖ Dark green floss
❖ Medium blue floss
❖ Purple
  scrapbooking chalk

Blue Blossom Ball

An instant antique—this project is a soft globe covered with nostalgic blue flowers and satin-stitched leaves. Aunt Martha would be proud!

1. Cut the following:
    ❖ 20 medium blue Pattern A triangles
    ❖ 20 light blue Pattern B triangles
    ❖ 20 cream Pattern C circles
2. With chalk, color sides of one light blue triangle as indicated. Repeat on remaining triangles and let dry.

3. Fold corners of light blue triangle to center, overlapping ends slightly. Place small cream circle in center, and with dark green floss, hand stitch to center of one medium blue triangle with French knot. (Refer to General Instructions for Embroidery Stitches, page 8.) Repeat for remaining triangles.

4. With light green floss, satin stitch leaves in corners of triangles where indicated on Pattern A. (Refer to General Instructions for Embroidery Stitches, page 9.)

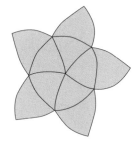

5. Whipstitch five decorated triangles together to make one pieced section, as shown in Diagram A.

Diagram A

6. Whipstitch five more decorated triangles to the first five triangles, as shown in Diagram B.

Diagram B

7. Repeat steps 5 and 6 to make a second pieced section. Both pieced sections should have 10 triangles each.

8. Wrap pieced sections around ball and whipstitch together, as shown in Diagram C.

Diagram C

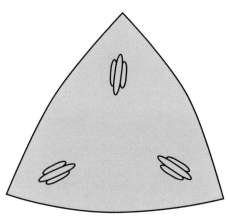

Pattern A

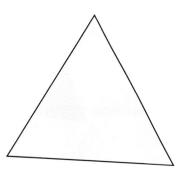

Pattern B

Pattern C

chapter seven

Turn the Tables

Tables are important sites in any home. A table is a place to drop belongings, to serve a meal, or to share an intimate conversation. Felt is a great drape for a table because the colors complement any decor and there is no hemming necessary.

❖ 1 yard purple wool felt (20% wool/80% rayon)
❖ 1⅛ yard navy blue felt
❖ Purple thread
❖ 2 stencil blanks or Mylar sheets (9" x 12")
❖ Stencil brush
❖ 2-oz. bottle periwinkle blue acrylic craft paint
❖ 2-oz. bottle medium green acrylic craft paint
❖ Craft knife
❖ Permanent marker
❖ Sewing machine
❖ Iron

All seam allowances are ¼".

Floral Tablecloth

One easy and effective way to add a pattern to almost anything is by stenciling. Stenciling is done with a template that has had the design area cut out and removed. This negative space is then filled in with paint or ink to create an image. You can work quickly, slowing down only to wait for each repeat to dry. The fibrous nature of felt absorbs paint well and makes this process almost foolproof.

1. From blue felt, cut four 6½" x 37½" strips.

2. Referring to General Instructions for Stenciling, page 11, use permanent marker to trace Floral Tablecloth Stencil Pattern on facing page onto Mylar and cut stencil for flowers.

3. With blue paint, stencil flowers on felt strips with approximately 3" between repeats, for a total of 2⅔ repeats or eight flowers per strip. Let dry.

4. Using a separate piece of Mylar, trace and cut stencil for leaves, facing page.

5. With green paint, stencil leaves on felt strips. Let dry.

6. From purple felt, cut one 31" square.

7. Right sides together, machine stitch first strip to center square, stopping seam ¼" from edge of square, as shown in Diagram A. Press and continue with remaining strips.

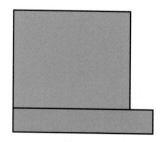

Diagram A

8. Tuck short end of last strip, under first strip. Complete seam from first strip, as shown in Diagram B and press.

9. Hand stitch running stitch on purple felt ¼" from seam, as shown in the photo below.

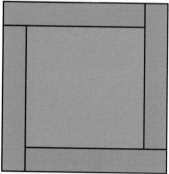

Diagram B

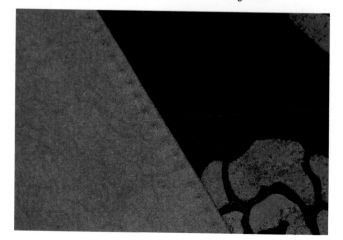

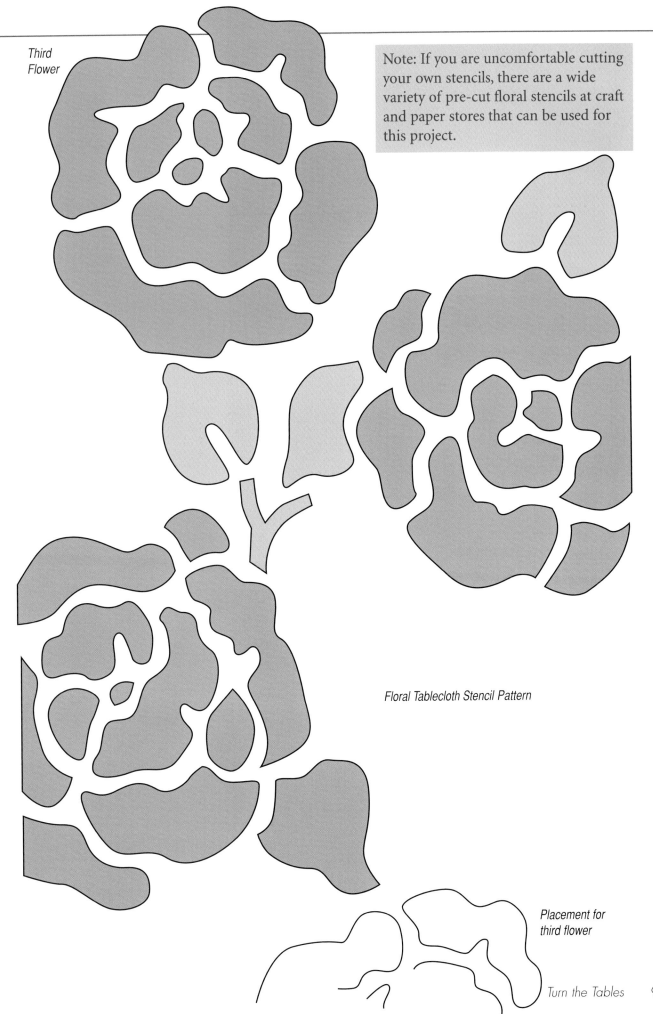

Third Flower

Note: If you are uncomfortable cutting your own stencils, there are a wide variety of pre-cut floral stencils at craft and paper stores that can be used for this project.

Floral Tablecloth Stencil Pattern

Placement for third flower

❖ 1 yard dusty pink felt
❖ ¾-yard gold satin fabric
❖ 1¼ yards fusible web
❖ 1 yard cream cotton fabric
❖ 2 yards rayon fringe
❖ 2⅛ yards twisted rayon cord
❖ Gold thread
❖ Sewing machine
❖ Iron
❖ Masking tape (optional)

All seam allowances are ¼".

Harlequin Tablecloth

The best thing about this tablecloth is the interesting contrast between the felt and the satin. Felt absorbs light and has a mat finish. Satin reflects light to appear shiny. This difference in surface texture makes for a rich and appealing tabletop decoration.

1. From pink felt, cut one 36" square.

2. On paper side of fusible web, trace 54 Pattern A diamond shapes on facing page, as shown.

3. Following manufacturer's directions, fuse web to wrong side of satin fabric.

4. Cut out diamonds, remove backing paper from each, and place on felt square, as shown in Diagram A. Cover entire felt square with diamonds.

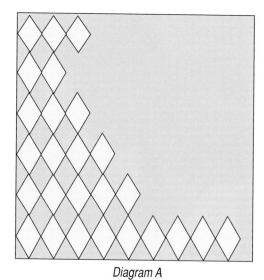

Diagram A

5. On synthetic setting of iron, carefully fuse diamonds to the felt.

6. Machine topstitch around each diamond, as shown.

7. From rayon fringe, cut two 35" lengths.

8. Turn fringe to inside of tablecloth on opposite ends, and matching bound edge of fringe to raw edge of pillow top, pin or baste in place. To secure fringe while machine stitching, tape or baste to right side of tablecloth.

9. From cotton fabric, cut one 36" square for tablecloth back.

10. Right sides together, machine stitch tablecloth top to tablecloth back, leaving 8" opening to turn. Trim excess fabric from corners. (Refer to General Instructions for Trimming Corners, page 10.)

11. Turn right-side out, remove tape or basting stitches, and whipstitch opening closed. Press.

12. Cut cord in half lengthwise.

13. Center one cord length on one fringed end of tablecloth and pin at edge. Knot ends to match corners and trim. With gold thread, whipstitch cord to edge of tablecloth over fringe.

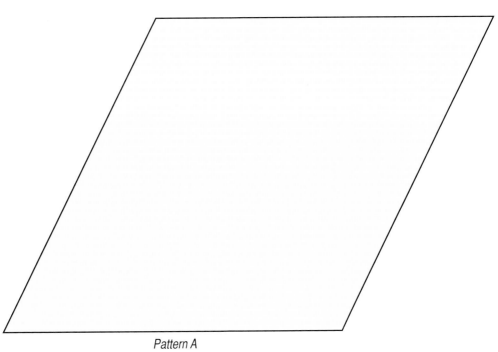

Pattern A

chapter eight

Play With Yo-Yos

Making yo-yo quilts have long been a popular way to use up precious fabric scraps. They are actually coverlets rather than quilts given that there is no layered batting or running stitches used. Cloth yo-yos are made from gathered circles of fabric that are arranged in a honeycomb or flower pattern and whipstitched together. Felt yo-yos are made from notched circles rather than complete circles. This shape eliminates bulk, and when the cut sides are gathered they create a rich sculpted texture.

- ❖ ½-yard cream felt
  (or five 9" x 12" cuts)
- ❖ 9" x 12" cut light turquoise felt
- ❖ ¾-yard periwinkle blue felt
- ❖ 1 square-yard cotton quilt batting
- ❖ Cream thread
- ❖ Turquoise thread
- ❖ Blue thread
- ❖ Sewing machine

All seam allowances are ¼".

Yo-Yo Pillow

This field of ivory and turquoise yo-yos looks as if it was squirted on this bolster pillows by a pastry chef.

1. From cream felt, cut 49 Pattern A shapes, as shown at right.

2. From turquoise felt, cut 10 Pattern A shapes. Note: Yo-yos on model cover only ⅔ of pillow surface. If you wish to cover entire surface make 80 cream yo-yos and 16 turquoise yo-yos. You may have to fill-in with a few extra, depending on how tightly they are spaced.

3. For cream yo-yos, with two strands of cream thread, insert needle from wrong side of one Pattern A shape, through each "petal" at dot, as shown here.

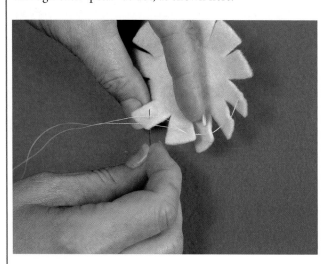

4. Pull length of thread tightly to form yo-yo, as shown below. Knot end to secure. Shape to make uniform.

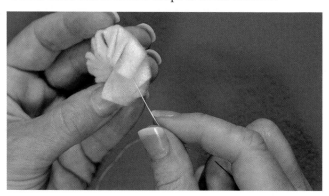

5. Repeat steps 3 and 4 for remaining 48 cream yo-yos.

6. For turquoise yo-yos, use turquoise thread and follow steps 3 and 4.

7. From periwinkle felt, cut one 12¾" x 20" rectangle and two 1½" x 19½" strips.

8. Fold strips in half lengthwise, match tops of strips to top of rectangle as shown in Diagram A, and with blue thread, machine stitch strips to 20" sides of rectangle.

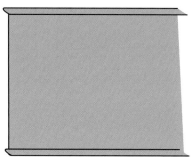

Diagram A

9. From periwinkle felt, cut two 3" x 19½" rectangles.

10. With blue thread, machine stitch two 3" x 19½" rectangles to center rectangle from step 8 along seams, as shown in Diagram B.

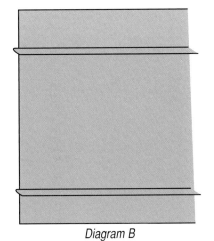

Diagram B

11. Pin yo-yos in place and with matching thread, whipstitch them to the felt, as shown in Diagram C.

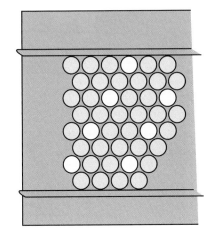

Diagram C

12. Fold sides of batting to center in thirds to measure 12" x 36".

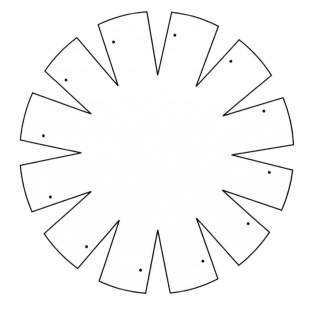

Pattern A

13. Staring at short end, roll snuggly to create cylinder pillow form 5" to 5½" in diameter and whipstitch batting edge to body of pillow to secure.

14. Matching side seams to edges of pillow form, wrap yo-yo-covered felt around tube. Overlap 12¼" sides and with blue thread, whipstitch seam closed, as shown here.

15. To close ends, make running stitch ¼" from edge and pull tightly.

16. With blue thread, whipstitch ends at centers to secure, as shown below.

- ❖ 2 cuts gold felt (each 9" x 12")
- ❖ 9" x 12" cut sage green felt
- ❖ ⅓-yard cobblestone wool felt (20% wool/80% rayon)
- ❖ Wood frame with 10" square window
- ❖ 10" square mat board
- ❖ Gold thread
- ❖ Craft knife
- ❖ Metal ruler
- ❖ Cutting surface
- ❖ White craft glue
- ❖ Masking tape
- ❖ Framing nails (optional)

Yo-Yo Frame

Yo-yos made from rich gold felt form a flowery border to show off an antique print.

1. Mark 5" square in center of mat board, as shown.

2. Place mat board on cutting surface, and using ruler as a guide, score along marked line, as shown. Repeat until window is cut from mat board. It will take several passes with the craft knife to cut completely through mat board. Hold ruler firmly in place throughout process.

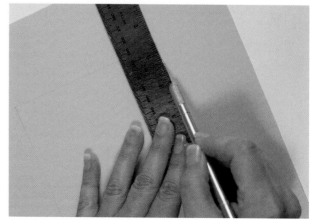

3. From tan felt, cut one 12" square. Cut a 3" window in center of the square. Cut diagonals in corners of window to 5" and then cut triangles from outer corners as indicated in Diagram A.

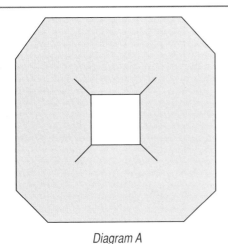

Diagram A

4. Place felt on work surface and then place mat on felt, as shown in Diagram B.

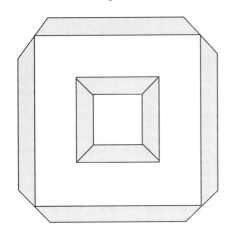

Diagram B

5. Apply thin layer of glue on mat board 1" around window.

6. Wrap edges of inside felt square to back of mat board around window, glue in place, and hold with tape until glue dries.

7. Apply thin layer of glue on mat board 1" around outside edge.

8. Wrap outside edges of felt to wrong side of mat board, glue in place, and hold with tape until glue dries.

9. From gold felt, cut 16 Pattern A shapes.

10. With two strands of cream thread, insert needle from wrong side of one Pattern A shape, through each "petal" at dot, as shown in step 3 of the Yo-Yo Pillow project, page 96.

11. Pull length of thread tightly to form yo-yo, as shown in step 4 of the Yo-Yo Pillow project, page 96. Knot end to secure. Shape to make uniform.

12. Repeat steps 9 through 11 for remaining 15 gold yo-yos.

13. From green felt, cut four leaf shapes with Pattern B.

14. Position one leaf shape in corner, as shown below, and glue in place. Repeat for remaining leaf shapes. Let dry.

15. Glue one yo-yo on each leaf shape. Place remaining yo-yos around frame window. Glue in place. Let dry.

16. Insert mat and artwork in frame and secure with tape or small framing nails.

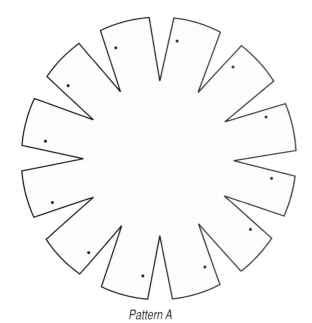

Pattern A

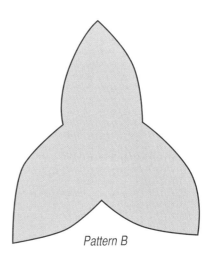

Pattern B

- ⅓-yard white felt
- 2 cuts dark turquoise felt (each 9" x 12")
- ¼-yard yellow felt
- ⅓-yard blue-and-white print cotton fabric
- ⅔-yard white cotton fabric
- ⅓-yard water-soluble stabilizer (such as Solvy)
- Water-soluble marking pen
- White thread
- Green thread
- Yellow thread
- Turquoise thread
- Sewing machine
- Iron

All seam allowances are ¼".

Yo-Yo Doll Quilt

Just add stems to these bright blue yo-yos and make a doll quilt that stays in bloom year-round.

1. From blue felt, cut 18 Pattern A shapes.

2. To make yo-yos, thread needle with two strands of turquoise thread and insert it through the wrong side of one Pattern A shape, through each "petal" at dot. Refer to the photo with step 3 of the Yo-Yo Pillow, page 96, for guidance.

3. Pull length of thread tightly to form yo-yo. Knot end to secure and shape to make uniform. Refer to the photo in step 4 of the Yo-Yo Pillow project, page 96, for assistance.

4. Repeat steps 2 and 3 for the remaining 17 turquoise yo-yos.

5. Cut the following:

- 25 3¾" squares from print fabric
- 24 3¾" squares from white felt
- 18 3¼" squares from stabilizer

6. Right sides together and using white thread, machine stitch together the print squares and the white felt squares, starting and stopping ¼" from ends of squares as shown in Diagram A to form a checkerboard background with print fabric corners. Press. (Refer to General Instructions for Trimming and Pressing Checkerboards, page 10.)

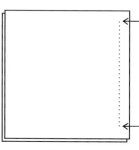

Diagram A

7. Place a stabilizer square diagonally over stem and leaf pattern. With top of stem in top left corner of square, trace pattern with marker. Repeat with remaining stabilizer squares.

8. On right side of quilt top, pin marked stabilizer squares onto white felt squares as shown in Diagram B.

Diagram B

9. Pin marked squares to 18 white felt squares. Do not pin marked squares to top row or to left row of white felt squares. Refer to project photo for guidance.

10. Adjust sewing machine to ⅛"-wide satin stitch, and with green thread, machine satin stitch over marked stems and leaves. Trim threads.

11. Carefully tear or trim away large areas of stabilizer. To remove remaining stabilizer, follow manufacturer's directions and submerge in water. Let dry and then press.

12. From white cotton fabric, cut one 23¼" square for the quilt back.

13. Wrong sides together, baste checkerboard quilt top to quilt back ¼" from edge.

14. From yellow felt, cut two 2" x 23¼" strips and two 2" x 26¾" strips.

15. Right sides together and with yellow thread, machine stitch the shorter 23¼" strips to opposite sides of quilt top, sewing through all layers. Do the same with the other two 26¾" strips for the remaining sides.

16. Cut ⅞" notches in corners of yellow felt binding, as shown in Diagram C.

17. Wrap yellow felt binding to back of quilt and with yellow thread, whipstitch in place along seam line, overlapping at corners.

18. With turquoise thread, whipstitch yo-yos to stem tops at corners.

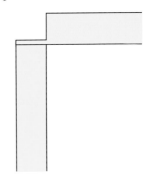

Diagram C

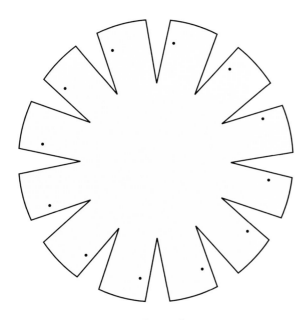

Pattern A

Leaf and Stem Pattern

chapter nine

Oh Baby

What is perhaps the most common use of felt in crafting is soft sculpture. It's soft compliant nature, and its crisp cut edges make it the perfect sculpting medium. And who is more deserving of a fuzzy hand-made creation than a baby?

The projects within this chapter are perfect for decorating a baby's nursery or the bedroom of a young child.

materials needed

- ❖ 2 cuts blue felt (each 9" x 12")
- ❖ 9" x 12" cut ivory felt
- ❖ 9" x 12" cut purple felt
- ❖ Ivory thread
- ❖ Orange thread
- ❖ Blue thread
- ❖ Purple thread
- ❖ Charcoal gray embroidery floss
- ❖ 6 ⅜" chenille balls
- ❖ Fiberfill
- ❖ 17" twig
- ❖ Air-soluble marking pen
- ❖ Sewing machine

Bunny Branch

These bunnies come to life almost instantly with a little hand stitching, a little machine stitching, and a little stuffing. Any baby would love to have this trio hanging around.

1. From ivory felt, cut the following:
   ❖ One head front with Pattern A, page 107.
   ❖ One head back with Pattern B, page 107.
   ❖ Two ⅝" x 4" strips for ears.

2. Starting at narrow end of each dart and with ivory thread, whipstitch darts on both head pieces, as shown. Stop stitching ³⁄₁₆" from end.

3. Fold each ⅝" x 4" ear strip in half lengthwise. Baste ends of ears to wrong side of head front, as shown below.

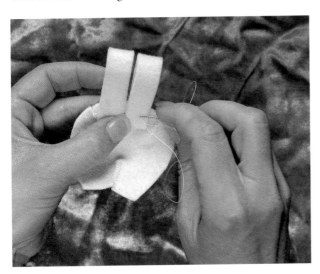

4. Wrong sides together, pin or baste head front to head back and with ivory thread, machine stitch together ³⁄₁₆" from edge. Remove basting stitches if necessary.

5. From blue felt, cut two body shapes with Pattern C, page 107.

6. Pin or baste body shapes together and with orange thread, machine stitch together ³⁄₁₆" from edge. Remove basting stitches if necessary.

7. Lightly stuff head with fiberfill, as shown below. Do the same for the body.

8. Tuck head into body, and with blue thread, whipstitch body to head, as shown here.

9. With marker, draw eyes, nose, and mouth on face, as shown in Diagram A.

Diagram A

10. Referring to General Instructions for Embroidery Stitches, pages 8 and 9, use two strands of charcoal gray embroidery floss to stitch face on head, as shown below. Use French knot stitch for eyes, satin stitch for nose, and long stitches for mouth.

12. Repeat steps 1 through 11 to make one more blue bunny and one purple bunny.

13. Thread twig through ears, as shown, and hang.

11. With ivory thread, hand stitch chenille balls onto toes.

Felt Art Accents For the Home

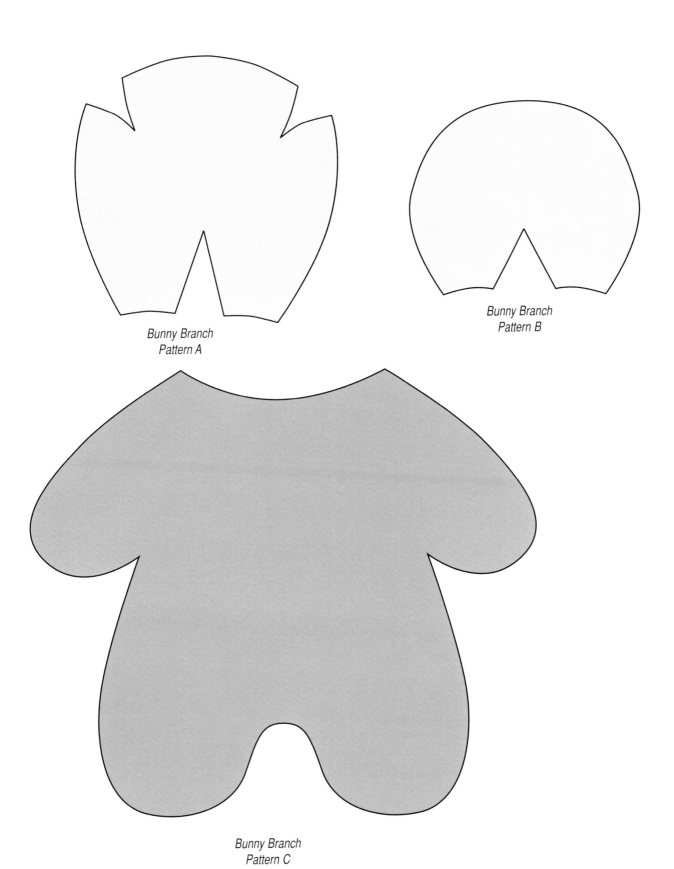

Bunny Branch
Pattern A

Bunny Branch
Pattern B

Bunny Branch
Pattern C

Sparkle Shoe Garland

Polish up plain ivory felt, with some powdery white glitter. All it takes to perform this magic is glitter, fusible web and a hot iron. Then use the dressed-up felt to make a pair of charming baby shoes. Float them over a doorway or drape them on top of a mirror.

1. From ivory felt, cut one 3" x 9" rectangle.

2. From fusible web, cut one 3" x 9" rectangle.

3. Following manufacturer's directions, fuse web to ivory felt rectangle. Let cool. Remove protective paper and set aside.

4. Place sheet of typing paper on ironing board and then place felt with fused web, exposed adhesive side up, on paper. Carefully sprinkle thin layer of glitter on exposed adhesive, as shown. Be careful: If glitter is too thick, it will flake off after ironing.

5. Discard typing paper and excess glitter.

6. Place protective paper from fusible web on glitter and with iron on "synthetic" setting, iron over paper to fuse glitter to felt, as shown. Let dry.

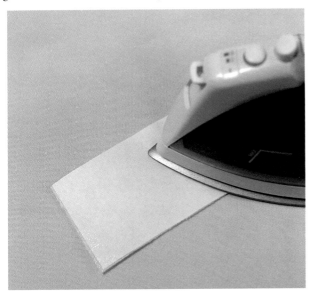

7. Remove protective paper, as shown below.

8. From glitter-coated felt, cut one left toe with Pattern A, page 110. Then reverse pattern and cut one right toe with Pattern A.

9. Hand stitch running stitch between dots on left toe and gather slightly. Repeat for right toe.

10. From ivory felt, cut one left sole with Pattern B, page 110. Then reverse pattern and cut one right sole with Pattern B.

11. Match gathered left toe to left sole and with closely spaced whipstitches, hand stitch together. Repeat for right toe and sole.

12. From ivory felt, cut two heels with Pattern C, page 110.

13. Match heels to souls, overlapping toe pieces at sides, and with closely spaced whipstitches, hand stitch together. Then with running stitch, hand stitch heel pieces to toe pieces at sides, as shown below.

14. From ivory felt, cut four ⅜" x 3" strips.

15. With closely spaced whipstitches, hand stitch two strips together to make strap and hand stitch to left shoe at ends. Repeat for right shoe.

16. With long stitches, hand stitch buttons on shoes, as shown at right.

17. Whipstitch shoes to white bead strand and hang.

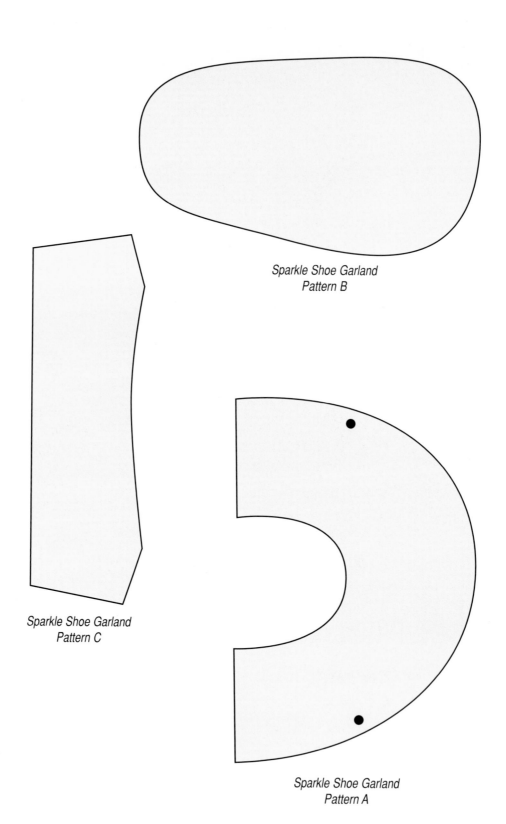

Sparkle Shoe Garland
Pattern B

Sparkle Shoe Garland
Pattern C

Sparkle Shoe Garland
Pattern A

❖ 9" x 12" cut ivory felt
❖ 1 small tube or package fine white glitter
❖ 3" x 9" rectangle fusible web
❖ Ivory thread
❖ Lavender thread
❖ 2 pink ⅜" buttons
❖ 1 sheet typing paper
❖ ⅓-yard lavender plush felt
❖ Fiberfill
❖ Sewing machine
❖ Iron

All seam allowances are ¼".

Sparkle Shoe Pillow

This pillow is the baby version of Cinderella's glass slippers displayed on a tapestry pillow. (Well almost, if you substitute glittery felt for glass and plush felt for tapestry.) This will be the favorite accent for a little girl who loves fairy tales, or for an older girl who hasn't quite outgrown them.

1. From ivory felt, cut one 3" x 9" rectangle.

2. From fusible web, cut one 3" x 9" rectangle.

3. Following manufacturer's directions, fuse web to ivory felt rectangle. Let cool. Remove protective paper and set aside.

4. Place sheet of typing paper on ironing board and then place felt with fused web, exposed adhesive side up, on paper. Carefully sprinkle thin layer of glitter on exposed adhesive, as shown at right. Be careful: If glitter is too thick, it will flake off after ironing.

5. Discard typing paper and excess glitter.

6. Place protective paper from fusible web on glitter and with iron on "synthetic" setting, iron over paper to fuse glitter to felt, as shown. Let dry.

7. Remove protective paper, as shown below.

8. From glitter-coated felt, cut one left toe with Pattern A, page 110. Then reverse pattern and cut one right toe with Pattern A.

9. Hand stitch running stitch between dots on left toe and gather slightly. Repeat for right toe.

10. From ivory felt, cut one left sole with Pattern B, page 110. Then reverse pattern and cut one right sole with Pattern B.

11. Match gathered left toe to left sole and with closely spaced whipstitches, hand stitch together. Repeat for right toe and sole.

12. From ivory felt, cut two heels with Pattern C, page 110.

13. Match heels to souls, overlapping toe pieces at sides, and with closely spaced whipstitches, hand stitch together. Then with running stitch, hand stitch heel pieces to toe pieces at sides, as shown here.

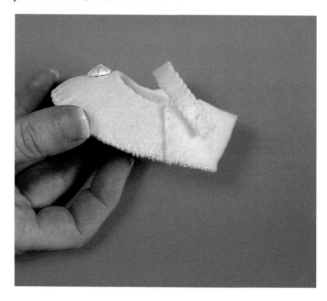

14. From ivory felt, cut four ⅜" x 3" strips.

15. With closely spaced whipstitches, hand stitch two strips together to make strap and hand stitch to left shoe at ends. Repeat for right shoe.

16. Hand stitch buttons to shoes.

17. From lavender plush felt, cut two 9 ½" squares for pillow top and back.

18. Right sides together and with lavender thread, machine stitch together leaving opening to insert fiberfill. Trim excess fabric from corners. (Refer to General Instructions for Trimming Corners, page 10.)

19. Turn right-side out, insert fiberfill, and whipstitch opening closed with lavender thread.

20. With ivory thread, hand stitch shoes to pillow top.

Heart Garland

Wear you heart on your sleeve—and perhaps on your window frame. Make these seven hearts, then sprinkle them with beads and stitch them to a string of pearls for a unique ornamental draping.

materials needed

- ❖ ¼-yard hot pink felt
- ❖ 9" x 12" cut ivory felt
- ❖ 9" x 12" cut dark green felt
- ❖ 1 package 4mm ivory beads
- ❖ Hot pink thread
- ❖ Ivory thread
- ❖ Fiberfill
- ❖ 1¼ yards pale pink pre-strung beads
- ❖ 2½ yards white pre-strung beads

1. From pink felt, cut 14 heart shapes with Pattern A, page 114.

2. Pin the two Pattern A heart shapes together and with pink thread, whipstitch together, leaving 2" opening on one side of heart to insert stuffing.

3. Lightly stuff heart with fiberfill and whipstitch opening closed.

4. Repeat steps 2 and 3 to make six more hearts.

5. From ivory felt, cut seven ⅜" x 5" strips.

6. Referring to the photos at right and the top of the next page, carefully tie each strip in single knot, trim ends, and with ivory thread, hand tack in place at back of knot to form rosebud. You should end up with seven rosebuds.

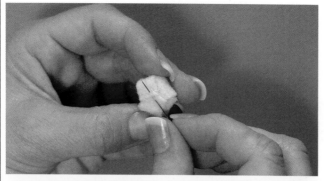

11. Whipstitch heart backs to white bead strand looping strand between hearts, as shown here.

7. From green felt, cut seven leaf shapes with Pattern B.

8. Place leaf shapes to center of "V" on each heart and then place one rosebud on each leaf. With ivory thread, hand tack rosebuds to hearts over leaf shapes.

9. Bring needle through heart backs, and hand stitch beads to heart fronts in random pattern.

10. Whipstitch heart backs to pink bead strand.

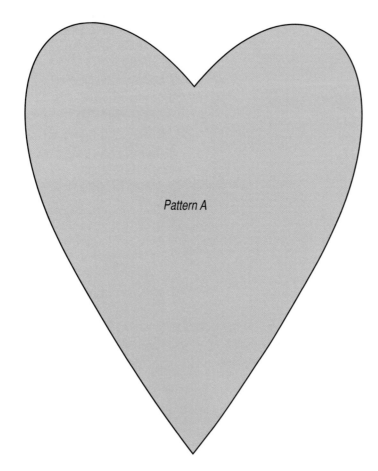

Pattern A

Pattern B

materials needed

❖ 2 cuts hot pink felt (each 9" x 12")
❖ 9" x 12" cut ivory felt
❖ 9" x 12" cut dark green felt
❖ Hot pink thread
❖ Ivory thread
❖ Fiberfill
❖ Embroidery floss in the following colors; purple, lavender, light pink, dark pink, red, and burgundy
❖ 13" twig

Cross-Hatched Hearts

Fine artists often create shadows and contrast with layers of overlapping lines called cross-hatching. These overlapping lines of floss are used instead to make an interesting pattern. Experiment with color, length, and number of lines. They can be stitched almost as fast as they can be drawn. Attach to a coarse twig to display.

1. From pink felt, cut six heart shapes with Pattern A below.

2. Pin the two Pattern A heart shapes together and with pink thread, whipstitch together, leaving 2" opening on one side of heart to insert stuffing.

3. Lightly stuff heart with fiberfill and whipstitch opening closed.

4. Repeat steps 2 and 3 to make two more hearts.

5. From ivory felt, cut three ⅜" x 5" strips.

6. Referring to the photos below, carefully tie each strip in single knot, trim ends, and with ivory thread, hand tack in place at back of knot to form rosebud. You should end up with three rosebuds.

7. From green felt, cut three leaf shapes with Pattern B.

8. Place leaf shapes to center of "V" on each heart and then place one rosebud on each leaf. With ivory thread, hand tack rosebuds to hearts over leaf shapes.

9. Using two strands of embroidery floss, stitch through surface of heart with long stitches, in random pattern to create cross-hatching, as shown.

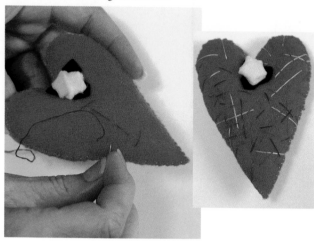

10. Whipstitch heart backs to twig and hang.

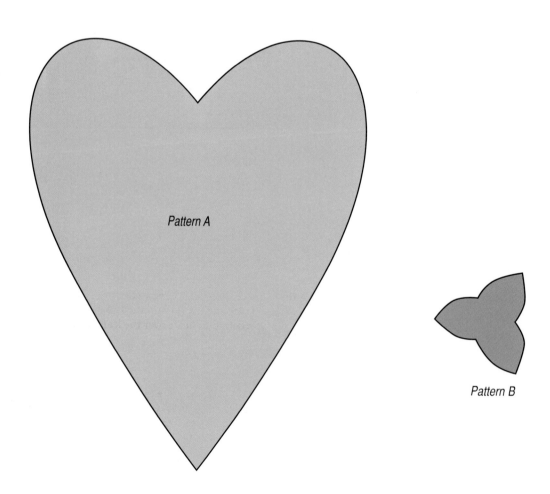

Pattern A

Pattern B

❖ ⅓-yard pale yellow plush felt
❖ 9" x 12" cut hot pink felt
❖ 9" x 12" cut ivory felt
❖ 9" x 12" cut dark green felt
❖ Ivory thread
❖ Hot pink thread
❖ Pale yellow thread
❖ Fiberfill
❖ Sewing machine

All seam allowances are ¼".

Heart Pillow

This fluffy pillow, sporting a bright pink heart, can serve as the perfect place to hide a baby tooth. But beware: The tooth fairy will be tempted to slip away with the tooth—and the pillow!

1. From pink felt, cut two heart shapes with Pattern A on the facing page.

2. Pin the two Pattern A heart shapes together and with pink thread, whipstitch together, leaving 2" opening on one side of heart to insert stuffing.

3. Lightly stuff heart with fiberfill and whipstitch opening closed.

4. From ivory felt, cut one ⅜" x 5" strip.

5. Referring to the photos below, carefully tie the strip in single knot, trim ends, and with ivory thread, hand tack in place at back of knot to form rosebud.

6. From green felt, cut one leaf shape with Pattern B, facing page.

7. Place leaf shape to center of "V" on the heart and then place the rosebud on the leaf. With ivory thread, hand tack rosebud to heart over the leaf shape.

8. From yellow plush felt, cut two 10" x 12" rectangles for pillow top and back.

9. Right sides together and with yellow thread, machine stitch together, leaving opening to insert fiberfill. Trim excess fabric from corners. (Refer to General Instructions for Trimming Corners, page 10.)

10. Turn right-side out, insert fiberfill, and whipstitch opening closed with yellow thread.

11. With pink thread, hand tack heart to pillow top.

❖ ⅓-yard lavender plush felt
❖ 9" x 12" cut yellow felt
❖ 9" x 12" cut blue felt
❖ 9 4mm ivory beads
❖ 15 pink bugle beads
❖ Yellow thread
❖ Lavender thread
❖ Fiberfill
❖ Sewing machine

All seam allowances are ¼".

Yellow Flower Pillow

Stitch up this pillow when you have your first occasion of spring fever. Bright yellow flowers peeking through a soft and foggy background will bring sunshine into your nursery.

1. From yellow felt, cut six flowers with Pattern A below.

2. Pin two Pattern A flowers together, and with yellow thread, whipstitch together, leaving small opening to insert fiberfill.

3. Lightly stuff flower with fiberfill and whipstitch opening closed with yellow thread.

4. Repeat steps 2 and 3 to make two more flowers.

5. From blue felt scraps, cut three centers with Pattern B below.

6. With yellow thread and stitching through all layers, hand tack blue centers to yellow flower centers.

7. Hand stitch ivory beads to flower centers.

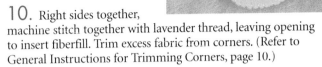

8. Hand stitch pink bugle beads to flowers, stitching through top layer of felt only, as shown at right.

9. From lavender plush felt, cut two 10½" squares for pillow top and back.

10. Right sides together, machine stitch together with lavender thread, leaving opening to insert fiberfill. Trim excess fabric from corners. (Refer to General Instructions for Trimming Corners, page 10.)

11. Turn right-side out, insert fiberfill, and whipstitch opening closed with lavender thread.

12. With yellow thread, hand stitch flowers to pillow top.

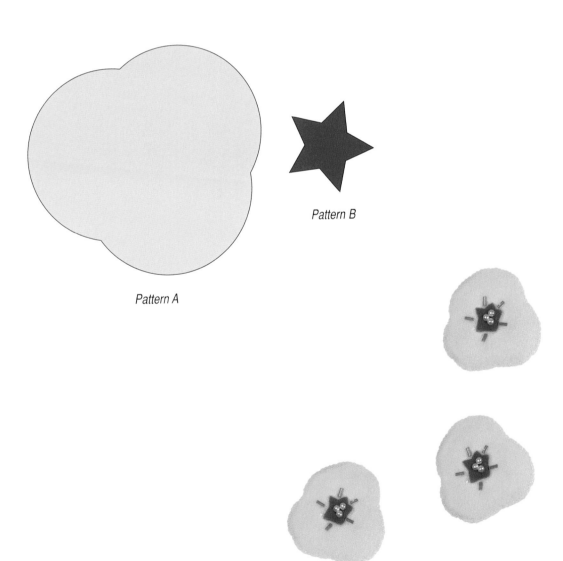

Pattern B

Pattern A

❖ ⅓-yard lavender plush felt
❖ 9" x 12" cut blue felt
❖ 1 small tube or package fine white glitter
❖ 4" square fusible web
❖ 1 sheet typing paper
❖ 4 white buttons (one ⁹⁄₁₆", three ⁵⁄₁₆")
❖ Blue thread
❖ Lavender thread
❖ Fiberfill
❖ Sewing machine
❖ Iron

All seam allowances are ¼".

Glitter Flower Pillow

Who can resist the dreaminess of plush felt? It is soft on the cheek and soft on the eyes as it is offered in an alluring palette of pastel colors. Make someone's dream come true by stitching up a plush pillow topped with a heart or some bright flowers.

1. From blue felt, cut one 4" square.

2. Following manufacturer's directions, fuse web to felt. Let cool. Remove protective paper and set aside.

3. Place sheet of typing paper on ironing board and then place felt with fused web, exposed adhesive side up, on paper. Carefully sprinkle thin layer of glitter on exposed adhesive. Be careful: If glitter is too thick, it will flake off after ironing. (See photo from step 4 of Sparkle Shoe Garland project, page 108, for assistance, if necessary.)

4. Discard typing paper and excess glitter.

5. Place protective paper from fusible web on glitter and with iron on "synthetic" setting, iron over paper to fuse glitter to felt. Let dry. (See photo from step 6 of Sparkle Shoe Garland project, page 108, for assistance, if necessary.)

6. Remove protective paper, as shown in step 7 of Sparkle Shoe Garland project, page 109.

7. Using Pattern A below, cut the following:
   ❖ One flower from blue felt.
   ❖ One flower from glitter-coated felt.

8. Pin two flower pieces together and whipstitch together with blue thread, leaving small opening to insert fiberfill.

9. Lightly stuff flower with fiberfill and whipstitch opening closed with blue thread.

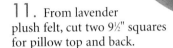

10. With blue thread, stitching through all layers, hand stitch buttons to flower center, as shown at right.

11. From lavender plush felt, cut two 9½" squares for pillow top and back.

12. Right sides together, machine stitch together with lavender thread, leaving opening to insert fiberfill. Trim excess fabric from corners. (See General Instructions for Trimming Corners, page 10.)

13. Turn right-side out, insert fiberfill, and whipstitch opening closed with lavender thread.

14. With blue thread, hand stitch flower to pillow top.

Pattern A

chapter ten

Felt Crazy

The favorite piecing style of the Victorians was the Crazy Quilt. Some were sewn together in a truly haphazard fahion. And some, like today's abstract art, were meticulously planned, with color, scale and balance as serious elements in the composition. Most Crazy Quilts sported bits of lace and a variety of embroidery stitches as accents.

Because of the constraints of space, this quilt is made by repeating one square. The wool felt, which is actually a blend of wool and rayon, has the look and feel of old wool, which was often used in these vintage quilts. The most unique characteristic of this modern Crazy Quilt is the shaded embroidery that is done with a very contemporary medium, designer scrapbook chalk.

❖ ⅔-yard purple wool felt (20% wool/80% rayon)
❖ ⅔-yard cream felt
❖ 9" x 12" scrap plum velvet
❖ ¼-yard light green velvet
❖ ¼-yard sage green cotton print fabric
❖ ¼-yard cream cotton print fabric
❖ ⅛-yard purple print cotton fabric
❖ ⅛-yard plum print cotton fabric
❖ ¼-yard olive green cotton print fabric
❖ 1⅓ yards yellow satin fabric
❖ Cream thread
❖ Gold thread
❖ 1¼ yards ⁷⁄₁₆"-wide metallic bias tape
❖ 1 yard ½"-wide gold lace trim
❖ 1⅓ yards ⅛"-wide gold grosgrain ribbon
❖ Black marking pen
❖ Tracing paper
❖ Air-soluble marker
❖ Lavender embroidery floss
❖ Dark green embroidery floss
❖ Purple scrapbooking chalk
❖ Green scrapbooking chalk
❖ Sewing machine
❖ Iron

All seam allowances are ¼".
Use cream thread for machine stitching unless otherwise indicated.

Crazy Quilt Wall-Hanging/Throw

Whether hung on a wall or thrown on a bed, this beautiful quilt is sure to add decorative flair to any room it graces. Remember quilts aren't just for bedrooms; think of hanging this nostalgic quilt in a hallway or in an entry.

1. From cream felt, cut a dozen 8" squares.

2. Using black marking pen, trace flower design from Diagram A, page 126, onto tracing paper. Place the design on a light table, or tape it to a window to assist in this step.

3. Noting angle of flower and using air-soluble marking pen, trace design onto 12 cream felt squares.

4. Using two strands of embroidery floss, embroider flowers, as shown in Diagram B. (Refer to General Instructions for Embroidery Stitches, pages 8 and 9.)

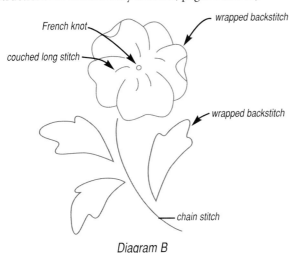

Diagram B

5. Cut the following:
   ❖ 12 Pattern A shapes, page 127, from embroidered cream squares
   ❖ 12 Pattern B shapes, page 127, from plum velvet
   ❖ 12 Pattern C shapes, page 127, from green velvet
   ❖ 12 Pattern D shapes, page 127, from sage green print fabric
   ❖ 12 Pattern E shapes, page 128, from cream print fabric
   ❖ 12 Pattern F shapes, page 128, from green velvet
   ❖ 12 Pattern G shapes, page 128, from purple print fabric

6. Right sides together, machine stitch B-shapes to A-shapes and press.

7. From gold lace trim, cut a dozen 2¼" lengths.

8. With gold thread, machine topstitch gold lace strips to Pattern B shapes where indicated on Diagram A, page 126.

9. From metallic bias tape cut, a dozen 3½" strips and machine topstitch to E shapes where indicated by broken line.

10. Referring to Diagram A for guidance, page 126, stitch pattern shapes C through F to squares in sequence and with right sides together. Press.

11. From plum print fabric scraps, cut a dozen ¾" x 3¾" strips.

12. Right sides together, machine stitch strips to G-shapes where indicated on Pattern G, page 128. Press.

13. Right sides together, machine stitch G shapes to pieced squares on side indicated on Diagram A. Press.

14. From gold grosgrain ribbon, cut a dozen 3½" lengths.

15. With gold thread, machine topstitch to squares, covering raw edges of plum print fabric with ribbon.

16. From purple felt, cut 13 6¾" squares.

17. Right sides together, machine stitch purple felt squares to pieced squares, starting and stopping ¼" from ends of squares, as shown in Diagram C. Form checkerboard with felt squares in corners. Press. (Refer to General Instructions for Trimming and Pressing Checkerboards, page 10.)

Diagram C

18. Color in sections of flower designs with chalk, as shown at right.

19. From olive print fabric, cut four 2" x 34¾" strips for border.

20. Right sides together, center strips to sides of checkerboard and machine stitch these strips to checkerboard, starting and stopping seams ¼" from ends. Miter corners. (See General Instructions for Mitered Corners, page 10.) Press.

21. From yellow satin fabric, cut a dozen 2" x 37¾" strips for border.

22. Right sides together, center yellow satin strips to olive green print strips and machine stitch strips together, starting and stopping seams ¼" from ends. Miter corners. Press.

23. From yellow satin, cut one 37¾" square for back.

24. Right sides together, machine stitch front to back, leaving 7" opening to turn. Trim excess fabric from corners. (Refer to General Instructions for Trimming Corners, page 10.)

25. Turn right-side out, whipstitch opening closed, and press.

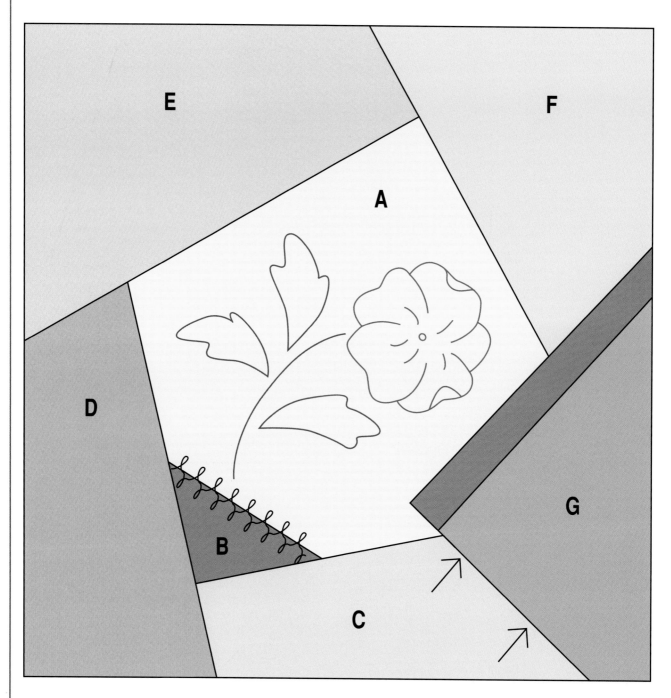

Crazy Quilt
Diagram A

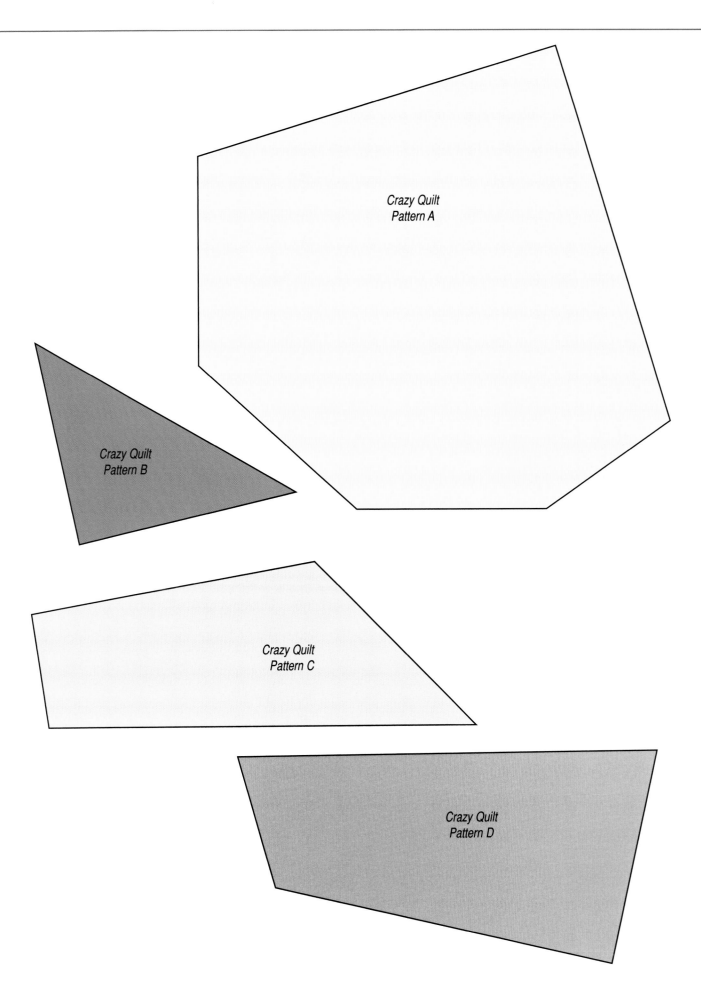

Crazy Quilt
Pattern A

Crazy Quilt
Pattern B

Crazy Quilt
Pattern C

Crazy Quilt
Pattern D

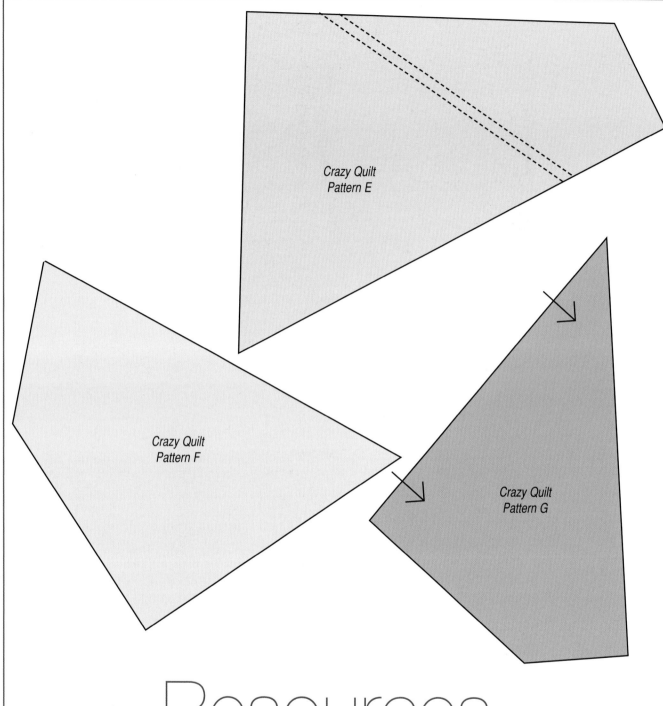

Crazy Quilt
Pattern E

Crazy Quilt
Pattern F

Crazy Quilt
Pattern G

Resources

CPE Inc.
P.O. Box 649
541 Buffalo
Union, SC 29379
Phone: (864) 427-7900
Fax: (864) 427-7904
Web site: www.cpe-felt.com

Kunin Felt
380 Lafayette Road
Hampton, NH 03842
Phone: (603) 929-6100
Fax: (603) 929-6180
Web site: kuninfelt.com

National Nonwovens
P.O. Box 150
Easthampton, MA 01027
Phone: (413) 527-3445
Fax: (413) 527-0456
Web site:
nationalnonwovens.com